MILLENNIUM

THE 1000 YEAR REIGN OF KING JESUS

BY

GEORGE OTIS SR.

ALBURY PUBLISHING
Tulsa, Oklahoma

Millennium: The 1000 Year Reign of King Jesus
ISBN 1-57778-127-9
Copyright © 2000 by George Otis Sr.
696 Verdemont Circle
Simi Valley, California 93065

Published by ALBURY PUBLISHING
P. O. Box 470406
Tulsa, Oklahoma 74147-0406

CONTENTS

MILLENNIUM

DEDICATION

PREFACE

"**Millennium:** Literally a period of a thousand years, (a pseudo-Latin word formed on the analogy of biennium, triennium, from Lat. *mille* a thousand, and *annus,* year.) The term is specially used to designate the period of 1,000 years during which Christ, as has been believed, would return to govern the earth in person. Hence it is used to describe a vague time in the future when all flaws in human existence will have vanished, and perfect goodness and happiness will prevail.

"Faith in the nearness of Christ's Second Advent and the establishing of his reign of glory on the earth was undoubtedly a strong point in the primitive church.

"Revelation 20 describes it this way: After Christ has appeared from heaven in the guise of a warrior and vanquished the anti-Christian world power, the wisdom of the world and the devil, those who have remained steadfast in the time of the last catastrophe and have given up their lives for their faith, shall be raised up and shall reign with Christ on this earth as a royal priesthood for 1,000 years. At the end of this time Satan is to be let loose again for a short season; he will prepare a new onslaught, but God will miraculously destroy him and his hosts. Then will follow the general resurrection of the dead, the last judgment, and the creation of new heavens and a new earth."

INTRODUCTION
THE ELECTRIC PRIEST

*The man's a fool and I'm tuning him out! It grates me to have
to sit here and listen to a layman trying to teach on, of all things,
Millennium life. No clergyman should ever be subjected to this
indignity from a layman.* Thus went the thoughts of the fuming
Catholic priest during a meeting many years ago in Auckland,
New Zealand.

Father John had been brought to the meeting from his parish,
70 miles south. He looked around the audience in College
Meeting Hall and thought, *Why, these people are spellbound!
They're swallowing the man's teaching, even though he confessed
never having gone to seminary. Out from under clergy's control,
these laymen's meetings can be dangerous. They seem to let anyone
teach, and on just about anything at all. Besides, there just isn't
much in the Bible about that era. The Millennium idea is so
ethereal; why doesn't he stick to things that will help people now?*

Father John nudged the parishioner who had talked him
into coming to Auckland on his Sunday afternoon off to hear

this George Otis, and said, "Let's get out of here. This man is trying to teach on something no one knows about. The Millennium, huh! Come on, let's head back home."

His friend said, "Shhh! I'd like to hear the rest. It's really interesting! Please hold on."

The priest slumped back in the chair with his arms tightly folded and fumed until I had finished my message.

Monday dawned as one of those bright New Zealand sparklers. At the breakfast table, Father John's thoughts turned back to his experience in last night's meeting. His repugnance had somehow grown even further during the night. John knew he should dismiss the whole episode from his mind, but there was something gripping about what he had heard concerning the Millennium. Talking to the air, he said, "Just imagine the impudence of a layman spouting Scripture and trying to interpret it to me, a man of the cloth. Laymen need the guidance of proven scholars."

Later that morning in the rectory, Father John opened his Bible. His eyes fell on 2 Peter 1:20. The words struck like fire! **Knowing this first, that no prophecy of the scripture is of any private interpretation.** He slammed the book shut and sat there transfixed. God seemed to be shouting to him, "My holy Word is a direct communication to each of My children! I am prepared to interpret Scripture for any sincere believer, clergyman or otherwise!"

Father John thought, *Otis used that very same scripture yesterday! Strange I should stumble over a verse I never noticed before.*

The following afternoon, the priest was at his desk in the rectory library. He drew from the shelf a volume on St. Francis of Assisi, one of the most towering and classic of Roman Catholic heroes. St. Francis had always been an inspiration to Father John.

Some twenty minutes later, the priest flinched. St. Francis, sharing about his own personal relationship with birds and animals, wrote of a deep stirring in people to make friends with wild things and how he believed this was a subconscious vestige from Eden days when Adam had joyous communion with the animals. St. Francis said he believed that in the Millennium there would be a restoration of man's fellowship with all creation.

St. Francis teaching on the Millennium? mused the puzzled clergyman. He was awestruck! He had just pooh-poohed this same concept in George Otis' message! The layman's revelation had been identical to one of his own revered saint. It was haunting, but still irritating.

This Protestant must have lucked out in this part of his teaching, Father John thought. *What does all this mean anyhow? Is God trying to say something to me?* He brushed it aside as mere coincidence, and his anger toward the layman's teaching remained.

The next day the priest looked at his calendar. It was Wednesday. He strode across the lawn and up the church steps. Father Roland greeted him just inside the sanctuary. "Good morning, Father John, I have a favor to ask. We have chosen you to represent the parish at a meeting downtown in the

Fellowship Hall tomorrow noon. There's a speaker in town for just one day and all faiths are collaborating in his meetings. It would be rude if our parish were not represented."

Father Roland handed Father John a folded yellow bulletin and said, "The time and particulars are printed on here, John. I appreciate your fulfilling this obligation for us." The priest slowly straightened out the bulletin and turned it over—he nearly dropped it!

One Day Only!
Presbyterian Layman From U.S.A.
Meeting Times: 12 Noon & 7 P.M.
All Denominations Welcome!
Admission Free
Speaker: George Otis

Father John was speechless! This was getting ridiculous.

It was high noon on Thursday when Father John steamed into Fellowship Hall. About a hundred special guests had gathered for the luncheon meeting. Prominent businessmen, pastors, and others waited to hear the speaker. Quickly the priest spotted his irritator standing in the midst of a cluster of people. The redheaded Catholic set a straight course for the group like a destroyer at full speed.

He broke in, "Mr. Otis, my name is Father John. I was one of the people in your audience last Sunday evening in Auckland."

I turned to the priest and thrust out my hand. "Were you, really? It's good to meet you formally. Do you live in this city, Father?"

Father John never took my hand or answered my question. Instead he continued to speak. "It would be less than honest if I didn't tell you how disturbed I was with your teaching on the Millennium. As a matter of fact, it has hung over me all this week. I'm here only because I was ordered to represent our parish.

"Mr. Otis, I'm a blunt man; and you should know I couldn't, in good conscience, come here. I don't agree with your teaching; furthermore I felt it was presumptuous for a layman to try to teach when there were clergymen in the audience. Bible information on the Millennium era is too sketchy for even a trained theologian to handle. Frankly, I was offended by your brashness in tackling such a hazy and delicate subject."

The priest's onslaught horrified the other New Zealanders standing around me. One by one they began to melt away. Soon the two of us were left standing alone in the center of the room, while the rest kept a courteous distance.

Looking at Father John, I replied, "Father, I simply don't know what to say. I'm so sorry to have offended you. My wife and I are only in your country in response to an invitation from some New Zealanders to come and minister. Now, as regards this message of the coming Millennium, I have spent almost a year doing prayerful research through the Bible on this age. The message was laced with Scripture. I am very particular about accuracy. It grieves me that this has upset you so deeply."

Some ten minutes after Father John's unsettling words, I was asked to address the group. At that stage, I was so deeply wounded the Lord had to carry on with no help from me. It

13

was only by His strength and anointing that I was able to minister at all. The response following the meeting, however, encouraged me.

After greeting people individually, my wife, Virginia, and I headed out to the parking lot. While driving back to the home of our hosts, I began to share what Father John had said just before I spoke. The intensity of the priest's reaction to the Millennium teaching baffled us, and we started to pray as we rode along.

When it became my turn, I prayed along this line: "Dear Lord, thank You for this difficult experience. I know that all things work together for good. Please forgive me for my own bristling against his attack. But Lord, would You bring a troubling on Father John? Don't let him rest until this conflict is resolved. May there be a healing for his sake and for the cause of Christ. And would You somehow bring it about before we leave town? Thank You, Lord. Amen."

Our emotions were still pretty lacerated, so, after having promised our hostess that we would be back in time for dinner, Virginia and I borrowed the car and headed for the seashore. As we walked along the beautiful New Zealand coast, we soon felt a restlessness rising within us. The time at the beach didn't refresh us as we had hoped. I said, "Honey, let's go on back. This walk isn't doing anything for me."

Virginia agreed and we drove back through beautiful green hills, studded with thousands of fleecy sheep. When we wheeled into the driveway, our hostess came flying out to the car with her finger at her lips. She whispered, "Guess who's here. It's Father John. Can you believe it? I told him you wouldn't be back for a couple of hours, but he insisted on waiting. He's there, pacing back and forth, in the living room."

I said, "Good grief! This must be why we felt such a tug to come back ahead of schedule. I guess we hadn't expected the Lord to answer our prayer so quickly. Can you stall him for a few minutes? I need to collect myself and pray before I can face him. What's his mood?"

She said, "I don't know, but he seems pretty uptight."

Some ten minutes later I decided to face the music and headed for the living room. My voice cracked nervously as I stuck my head in the doorway, waved feebly, and said, "Good afternoon, Father. It's a surprise to see you here. Did you want to see me?"

After a cool greeting, he started another attack on the Millennium teaching. There came to me a strong sense to let him unload all his hard feelings. The verbal barrage rose to a peak, but after a few minutes it was as though his "anger batteries" began to run down. His final objections sputtered to a stop.

I said, "Father John, present-day Christianity is indebted to your late Pope John XXIII. When he encouraged Roman Catholics to study their Bibles and allow the Holy Spirit to move, it was like a fresh breeze blowing through a dank cathedral. Hundreds of vibrant Roman Catholics have encouraged me in various meetings around the world. Their contributions in praise and worship have been terrific. And their eagerness to believe that God is still a God of miracles has taught a lot of us Protestants something priceless."

The priest just stood there with a puzzled expression. Apparently he thought I was going to explode against his attacks on my message. It became obvious he was in the throes of inner conflict when he finally blurted out, "I am an arrogant man, and I can't stand it anymore! You have been humiliated and abused by me. It was hard to come here today, but there was a compulsion and I couldn't rest until I faced you. I was so agitated by what you had to say, and now I'm so miserable. Would you pray for me?"

The change was so unexpected it staggered me for a few seconds. Then I walked slowly across the room and laid my hands on his shoulders and looked into his face. When I started to pray, it was like a cloud lifted from us. I felt detached from the torrent of prayer coming from my own lips. The Lord was obviously with us and up to something.

The following half-hour was gloriously mind-blowing. Father John wanted prayer, and he got it. God's lightning had come to him! In vibrant sequence the magnificent priest spoke aloud the sinner's prayer; then prayed for a healing of his bitterness; then capped it all by praying for the power of the Holy Spirit. The thunder of God was at once beautiful and awesome! His prayers were answered with tears of joy. The troubled priest became gloriously electric!

A session of animated conversation followed. Finally I said, "Father, would you do something for me? I feel the Lord would be pleased if you'd lay hands on me before you go. There's a very heavy schedule before us here in New Zealand. Both Virginia and I would benefit by your prayers for us. Would you lay hands on me now and ask God's blessing? It would mean a lot to me, John."

His reaction was startling! In a swift recoiling motion, he stepped backward and said, "I can't pray like you do. No, no, I'm not worthy to lay hands on you! Please don't even suggest it."

What a change! Earlier the priest's intellect and his traditions had ganged up to create in him a terrible revulsion toward my teaching. A dark shadow had been cast in his mind over the realities of the Millennium era. After just an hour together, the Lord had beautifully changed the priest from a noisy negative to a dynamic positive. But now, he imagined that I was too holy for him to pray over! He felt unworthy to even lay his hands on me. He had swung much too far the other way.

I knelt and took his wrists, placing his hands right on the top of my head and said, "Father John, I insist that you pray for me right now. I need God's blessing through your prayers— don't rob me of this by getting a false feeling of my own holiness."

Father John dutifully spoke a few hesitant words and then a great dam broke! The power and presence of God came into that room like a flood. Never have I experienced prayer that so shook my soul! The prayer went on and on, and on…four minutes…five minutes…eight minutes. Finally I was squirming down there on my knees. Muscle cramps were coming into my legs. I started to laugh softly as Father John thundered on in prayer. First I couldn't get this priest to start praying for me, and now I couldn't get him to stop!

When I got up I was struck with the wonderful change in his countenance. I threw my arms around him and we both hopped around in a circle, laughing and crying. Never had I felt closer to any brother.

Now it was time for Father John to leave, and we headed arm-in-arm toward the door. Just before he reached for the knob, he turned and put his hand on my shoulder. He said, "George, I'm seeing something." Staring up at the ceiling with a misty expression, "It's as clear as real life, and it's wonderful."

I looked up at the ceiling and couldn't see anything. I asked, "What are you seeing, John? Tell me."

Father John said, "I see you and me sitting there on a big rock. It's during the Millennium, and we're talking. I'm nudging you and saying, 'Here we are, and it's real!' You know, George, you were right about the Millennium, after all!"

Chapter 1

The Most Important Choice in Life

Today we are heading for a place too wonderful to believe. Rejoice and dance, children of the Lord, for we are not citizens of this doomed world! We are not riding Satan's locomotive streaking toward hell. No way! The only destination for the Jesus train is heaven—and that station is coming up fast.

The Lord spoke about His heaven in fifty-three books of the Bible. It isn't just some figure of speech or some poet's concept. Heaven is a literal address for God and His angels. Heaven is an awesome and indescribable place that is so utterly glorious that even God can't fully describe it due to the limitations of our human language.

Eye hath not seen, nor ear heard, neither have entered into the heart of man, the things which God hath prepared for them that love him. 1 Corinthians 2:9

In heaven we will never be idle and we sure won't be bored! Never again will we know pain, sickness, aging, struggle, boredom, or fear. Moreover, it's interesting and wonderful that over the past few years we've been suddenly hearing of hundreds of people who died, went to heaven, but then returned to life. These people testify of what they saw in heaven before they were sent back.

They talk about crystal-clear air and the awesome magnitude of heaven, its never-before-seen lights and colors, its music, and the mind-boggling view of God's universe as they saw it from heaven. They tell that the stars, the moon, and the galaxies took their breath away. Each person said they had a glorious sense of being home at last. Their joy almost exploded upon reuniting with friends and loved ones who were there.

New flowers bloomed everywhere with countless new colors. Walking down those heavenly streets of gold and seeing the mansions in our Father's house awed them. The presence of our heavenly Father and Jesus gave a fragrance to everything everywhere.

Heaven has no need for locks, policemen, lawyers, doctors, or hospitals. Big lions and tiny little animals frolic together. And no one who has come back from heaven ever saw any blind, crippled, or aged. God promises, **Behold, I make all things new** (Revelation 21:5). Testimonies abound from those who talked with Jesus, and they tell how God's glory lights up all of heaven and music fills it.

LOOK OUT BELOW!

Heaven is coming up fast, and that's the best of news. However, there is also a wealth of Scripture, confirmed by many unsaved people who have returned from the dead, which tells about *hell*. The Lord declares that hell is as real and as eternal as heaven. It is a deep, deep pit of utter darkness, inhabited by tormenting spirits, crushing loneliness, and despair. The souls there are tortured by the realization that they are forever cut off from God, and they vividly remember how they could have avoided hell—a place where one can't even die—by receiving Jesus Christ as their Lord and Savior. Many of the witnesses to the horrors of hell gave their hearts to Jesus immediately upon their return to this life.

Today, we ride in a world with six billion other souls—a world that is streaking toward the finish line of time itself. The Lord has given us a powerful list of prophetic truths to insure that we can read the great clock of heaven that tells us the nearness of Jesus' return. He longs for every lost soul to embrace His cross and to enter His kingdom before that clock strikes midnight.

But *how much time is left?*

NOT MUCH!

Most Bible scholars agree that we are swiftly approaching the time when Jesus will return to earth—no longer the suffering Servant of Isaiah 53, but the triumphant King of Kings whom John saw during his revelation. At that moment, the war of all wars will end, the great clock of heaven will begin a

1,000-year countdown, and life on earth will change drasti-
cally. We will experience an intensity and quality of love not
known since Adam and Eve walked and talked with God in
the cool of the day because there will be no more Satan on the
earth! He and his evil hoard of demons will be bound for
1,000 years, and Jesus will rule from David's throne in Jerusalem
as God promised. (See Luke 1:32.)

But mark this down. After the Millennium is over, the
billions who have rejected salvation through Jesus Christ will
experience a cataclysmic crossroads from which there will be
no turning back. They will descend into a pit of thick darkness
out of which they can never return. There will be no friends to
keep them company ever again. They will be shattered as they
recall their rejection of Jesus' salvation and how they foolishly
thought hell was only a curse word. But worst of all, those who
descend into hell cannot even die.

What should we then do?

Don't let the sun set today without saying yes to Jesus!
Receive your passport to heaven direct from His nail-scarred
hands, and then go out to compel as many as you can to go
with you!

This most important life choice, heaven or hell, propels the
ministry of High Adventure to labor with an all-out intensity.
Only eternity will show the contributions being made at this
fleeting eternal moment. God has declared that even the
islands of the seas will come to know Jesus before the end of
time. Our radio arm, the Voice of Hope, broadcasts the Good

News of Christ's salvation to the nations, into every single continent and island and to the 200,000 ships at sea. We must send forth God's Word like golden rain and harvest every lost soul.

Everyone who has helped High Adventure has helped to create one of the great miracles for the final harvest. Its impact is staggering, but we should expect nothing less as we obey God in this Great Commission. We live by Jesus' powerful admonition:

I must work the works of him that sent me, while it is day: the night cometh, when no man can work. John 9:4

Chapter 2

Stranger Than Fiction

It will be so awesome it will be beyond words!

Jesus coming to earth and those early streaks of glorious light heralding the dawn of the Millennium will defy description! The Word tells us:

> *Eye hath not seen, nor ear heard, neither have entered into the heart of man, the things which God hath prepared for them that love him.* 1 Corinthians 2:9

This promise certainly includes the 1,000-year reign of Jesus. Brace yourself as we run and skip through the Millennium. If the realities of Millennium life seem too good to be true, don't let them stagger you. We will have to be remade to understand and to withstand its glories:

> *But we all, with open face beholding as in a glass the glory of the Lord, are changed into the same image from glory to glory, even as by the Spirit of the Lord.* 2 Corinthians 3:18

If this account seems like a science fiction fantasy, keep cool! *Truth really is stranger than fiction!* God communicates this same truth to us in His Word:

> *For my thoughts are not your thoughts,*
> *neither are your ways my ways, saith the Lord.*
> *For as the heavens are higher than the earth,*
> *so are my ways higher than your ways, and*
> *my thoughts than your thoughts.* Isaiah 55:8-9

It is a strange paradox that enlightened man, even at the turn of this millennium, is so poorly informed about this looming age. Though we are now veterans of the space age, many believers still hold such narrow perspectives—preoccupied with the sensual, the transitory, focusing on the things that can be seen, heard, touched, smelled, or tasted. It's like, "Me and my little world of the now."

Even so, deep inside each of us there is a built-in *knowing* whereby we have a sense of eternal existence, a subconscious realization that death is but a vehicle into another plateau of continuing life. The poet Henry Wadsworth Longfellow caught it in "The Psalm of Life":

> *Art is long and time is fleeting*
> *and the grave is not its goal...*
> *Dust thou art to dust returnest*
> *was not spoken of the soul.*

The mere three-score-and-ten years of this phase of our existence is so brief when compared with forever. What could be more relevant than to explore that future? So let's raise our vision far above natural horizons and survey the Millennium era.

Godly teachers have, in recent years, illuminated the two other pivotal events soon to occur: the Rapture (1 Thessalonians 4:16-17) and the Tribulation era. By now we have a pretty keen sense of both. But why are we still so foggy-minded about the great age that immediately follows them? The Millennium has always seemed so hazy, almost like a fairy tale, hasn't it? And we've tended to get it scrambled around in our thinking with heaven and eternity. Have you ever wondered about the coming thousand-year "Superworld"?

- What will we look like?
- Who will be here on earth during the Millennium?
- Will we see the saints of the past?
- What will be our relationship to the millions of non-Christians still alive after Armageddon?
- Will there be births and deaths?
- Will everyone be the same age?
- Will we just rest and play the harp?
- Will we ever visit other planets?
- What will our day-to-day life be like?

Great questions, aren't they? Well, by the time we have cruised through this book, these and scores of other Millennium questions will have been answered.

Perhaps this dearth of Millennium teaching, until now, stems from a divine strategy of timing. The books of Isaiah, Daniel,

Zechariah, and Revelation were unfathomable to those of prior generations—like so much gobbledygook, so puzzling and resistant to understanding. Yet those believers of the past sensed their mysterious messages were deeply meaningful.

Why then was their content so hard to crack? The writings of God are often like coded messages—for believers only. Jesus' parables carried secrets for the privileged ears of His followers. They once asked Him, "Why do You speak to them in parables?" Jesus answered,

Because it is given unto you to know the mysteries of the kingdom of heaven, but to them it is not given. Matthew 13:11

And in 1 Corinthians 2:14, Paul tells us,

But the natural man receiveth not the things of the Spirit of God: for they are foolishness unto him: neither can he know them, because they are spiritually discerned.

Jesus described a myriad of conditions that would all impact *one particular generation,* those who endure the end times. Looking down through the corridor of time, He saw those who would be alive when the curtain of this age would close. I believe we are that generation which Jesus saw and spoke about. And so, right on cue, we are experiencing the death throes of the age.

It's little wonder interest in end-time prophecies has exploded. Like a divine kaleidoscope, ancient Scriptures have

blazed out in new clarity. Even so, not just anyone will understand millennial secrets:

For the words are closed up and sealed till the time of the end....
And none of the wicked shall understand;
but the wise shall understand. Daniel 12:9-10

The Lord deposited scriptural veins of prophecy; we now
mine for knowledge as He fulfills the prophecies before our
eyes. What could better demonstrate that our world isn't some
rudderless ship driven by winds of accident? What better way
to prove the haunting accuracy of the Bible? God laid prophecies like deposits of gold, then covered them for such an hour
as this. He said,

Daniel, shut up the words, and seal the book,
even to the time of the end. Daniel 12:4

He then wrote clear instructions as to their uncovering in
the proper day:

And in that day shall the deaf hear the words of
the book, and the eyes of the blind shall see out
of obscurity, and out of darkness. Isaiah 29:18

Why, of course! Since we are the believers these scriptures
refer to, the time has now arrived for understanding of not only
the Rapture and the Tribulation, but also of millennial life.

SECRET SHARING

Several years ago, a strong impression came into my thoughts. It went something like this: *Life is becoming increasingly complex as the present age stutters to a close. Believers will often know fear, discouragement, and even times of hopelessness. The remaining days will grow more treacherous, yet it is so very important that no believer falter just before reaching the prize of the high calling, that not one fall through despair just a few feet— a few heartbeats—from the finish line.*

It is urgent that a clearer view of the glittering millennial prize be flashed on the screen of their understanding; to encourage and to steel believers, that none become castaways so close upon the Millennium.

Strengthen ye the weak hands, and confirm the feeble knees.
Say to them that are of fearful heart,
Be strong, fear not. Isaiah 35:3-4

One of the reasons I am releasing this new, updated version of my previous book, *Millennium Man,* is to encourage, strengthen, and give hope to Christians in these last days. Knowing we have such a glorious time ahead of us makes our present difficulties easier to bear!

For our light affliction, which is but for a moment,
worketh for us a far more exceeding and
eternal weight of glory. 2 Corinthians 4:17

CHAPTER 3

THE AGONY AND THE ECSTASY

His congregation roared when the preacher said, "I am trying to unscrew the inscrutable!" It was only partly funny to me because I could truly empathize. As the inspiration struck to write this book, little did I know of the dragons I'd encounter along the way. Monsters of fear, futility, and despair snarled at most every paragraph! Days of poring over Scripture blurred into weeks and months. But my ongoing pursuit of the Millennium's truths and realities was fueled by periodic scintillation as millennial verses began to flash open their secrets.

The enormous potential of unveiling this coming age was compelling throughout the writing. My vision for the work loomed like a huge block of granite, approached by a sculptor with chisel and hammer. Only God could see Michaelangelo's exquisite *Pieta* buried in the massive rock. Could he ever unlock her? Only absolute precision and delicacy would avoid mutilating her substance while cleaving away the extraneous.

Had the sculptor also trembled as he approached the raw block? Oh yes, I'm sure he did.

Could we ever unveil the scope of the Millennium in our day? If ever we could, believers would never again be quite the same! Yet the task seemed overwhelming. The kingdom age Scriptures are so strung out as to appear hopelessly entwined. They are commingled with heaven, the latter perfect age, natural kingdoms, and the kingdom of God within each believer. They describe a kingdom within several other kingdoms.

Early one morning while I was laboring over the manuscript, a spiritual note sounded to "write about the presence of God's glory during the new era." It was like a thunderclap! I immediately sensed this presence would change the whole planet's atmosphere from negative to positive. It presented a glittering new aspect of millennial life, and yet, how could I ever express it?

After hours of prayer and pondering I could still think of no way to describe this glory except by the word *glory* itself. How do you describe the indescribable—the infinite?

With all of Gertrude Stein's eloquence, even she felt semantically stifled at times. In one moment of rhapsody, she struggled to share the mystery and the ecstasy of a rose. But alas, it dwelt just beyond her reach to write down what she had so clearly seen in her heart. Finally, in exasperation Gertrude scrawled, "A rose, is a rose, is a rose."

The limitations of compassing supernatural truth while working with the crude tools of natural language can be painful at times! From time to time my head pounded as I stretched to paint an accurate word-picture of the Millennium.

During one segment I paced the office floor in frustration, trying to get something down on the Glory-of-God effect. Finally, after two days of writing, I was looking at fewer than 300 words. In disgust I cried, "Dear God, I am such a fool— walking in here where theologians are too wise to tread! I'm so ignorant and so unproductive. Why, oh why is this book so hard?!"

Within seconds a response rang back through my mind. It was gentle: "Don't be too harsh with yourself. While on earth, didn't I know the trials of expressing the inexpressible? I too felt limited by the dimensions of natural language in transmitting the supernatural, so I taught intricate spiritual mysteries through parables: 'The kingdom of God is like....'

"My son, be comforted. It is now time to further open millennial truths—it is time to demythologize My coming kingdom age. It will be especially profitable for My own during these darkening hours before the dawn. I have written, **In that day shall the deaf hear the words of the book, and the eyes of the blind shall see out of obscurity, and out of darkness** (Isaiah 29:18)."

CHAPTER 4

THE EDGE OF TIME

One day, as Jesus sat with an intimate circle of His disciples, they began to ask about things to come. Man has long sought to pull back the curtain of tomorrow, and those close to Jesus felt at liberty to query Him about the future. Like the disciples of old, we will look to the only accurate source of information about our future:

> *The secret things belong unto the Lord our God:*
> *but those things which are revealed belong unto*
> *us and to our children for ever.* Deuteronomy 29:29

It's *where* men turn for their information that counts. People lose millions of dollars acting on tips from undependable sources about the future in the stock market and horse races. Faulty information can cause great loss. Just as courts of law always gauge the reliability of evidence, so must we be sure of the trustworthiness of our millennial information because our destiny hinges on it.

Millions of marriages have been destroyed by sheer gossip. Bloody wars have exploded when momentous decisions were made on faulty intelligence. For Christians, it is a life-or-death matter that we heed the Word of God in our own life decisions.

Millions are spent trying to look into the future through wrong means, such as the occult. Pharaoh wasn't the only politician who staffed his court with seers. Several present-day leaders have been known to employ occult means in their governing processes. Some heads of corporations think it fashionable to inquire of fortunetellers to assist in their decision-making. Hundreds of thousands consult their horoscopes in daily newspapers and call 1-900 psychic lines each day. The consequences to humanity from these occult practices are often mental illness, bondage, and even suicide. Dabbling in tomorrow can be a risky business for the universe.

Present-day fascination with the occult stems from man's quest to know future events before they happen. Being the arch-opportunist, Satan has played on this curiosity for thousands of years. The Tower of Babel was used for ancient astrological efforts. For this abomination God fragmented humanity by confounding its speech. (See Genesis 11:1-9.)

In view of all this wreckage caused by seeking knowledge of the future from forbidden sources, you would think man would wise up. But don't hold your breath! King Saul couldn't wait to find out how the war he was fighting would turn out.

During the night he stole out of camp to ask the Witch of Endor. Saul got an answer all right. Along with the occult revelation, the prophet Samuel revealed to Saul that he was under severe judgment. The very next day a decapitated Saul hung by his heels, twirling in the sun. (See 1 Samuel 28:7-19.)

How foolish is mankind! When will we acknowledge the Bible as the perfect "fortune-telling" book? Does that shock you? Well, the semantics might shake us up, but let's face it—the Bible is the one and only dependable look into the future. With just this Book, any sincere person can accurately learn his own destiny, good or bad. It does not reveal just a few irrelevant tidbits from some fake crystal-ball gazer, nor does it give just a few bones from a seance. The Bible reveals mankind's entire panoramic future.

"But why trust *that* Book?" The Bible has taken more ridicule from the academic world than any book in history. It has been called sheer mythology, inaccurate, and even foolish. But its message has proven indestructible. The more it's attacked, the brighter it shines. It contains hundreds of insights to history written before the events took place. Nearly one-fifth of this Book is prophetic.

The Bible authenticates itself. Archaeologists have been utterly astounded recently by the accuracy of its record of past civilizations. Modern scholars acknowledge that it has often been ahead of science. Back when men were saying that the world was flat, the Bible said, **It is he** [God] **that sitteth upon the circle of the earth** (Isaiah 40:22).

The Bible's history-written-in-advance has awed godly scholars by its perfect batting average. Most of the prophecies about
men, cities, and nations have already come to pass exactly *how*
and precisely *when* the Bible said they would. These events
have marched right out of prophecy and into our history
books. This majestic parade of prophetic fulfillment proves
that humanity lives under divine management.

Yes, the Bible is an accurate book of fortune. So let's find out
about our own future from the One who controls that future.

> *For the prophecy came not in old time by the will*
> *of man: but holy men of God spake as they*
> *were moved by the Holy Ghost.* 2 Peter 1:21

Jesus foretold the circumstances we now see all about us. As
we read the Bible's account of our day, it's like reading *Time*
magazine. He wanted His followers to know when civilization
had arrived at the edge of time. We are the generation about
whom Jesus said,

> *And when these things begin to come to pass,*
> *then look up, and lift up your heads; for*
> *your redemption draweth nigh.* Luke 21:28

Before we travel into the world of the future, let's synchro-
nize our watches with the great clock in heaven. It's not easy
to believe we're standing at the end of this age. Everything looks
as though it will go on and on. Though our world is experiencing wars, crises, and discouragement, we are still getting along

pretty well. We're still building, buying, and marrying. Some say, "Hasn't the world always had problems?" Jesus said there would be those who wouldn't believe the end was near. But Christians can see these things through spiritual eyes.

Charles Duncombe wrote in *Christ for the Nations* magazine,

> The signs of history's approaching climax are multiplying. A few years ago those of the academy predicted that the salvation of the human race would soon be achieved through the magic of man's mind. Their prophecies of Utopia have faded. Their bright pictures have been darkened by the clouds of pessimism and what one writer called "irritated futility".
>
> Each year closes with the usual parties, fireworks, whistles and bell ringing, but they sound out over our cities crippled with brown-outs and fuel short-ages and sickened with crime.
>
> For the Christian, however, one magnificent and radiant star shines in the dark sky: He knows that these world pains are the birth pangs of a brand-new age, which is about to be born. The hands once nailed to a cross are about to seize the reins of human government. We are now praying with added excitement, "Thy Kingdom come"!

Jesus told us how our present generation would face condi-tions similar to those that occurred before the great flood. God, through Noah, had warned the sin-mad people. For years Noah urged the people to believe God and escape the coming judgment. He pleaded with them to heed the Word of a compassionate God who desired that they repent and thereby survive the coming deluge. But they scoffed, branding old Noah a doomsday crackpot. They blew him off as a religious fanatic.

The pre-flood philosophers, like many today, assured the people they needn't lose sleep over Noah's doomsday warnings. They went on doing their own thing up to the first ominous drops of rain.

Here we go again at the turn of the century! The Lord has prepared the ark of salvation. He is calling earth's people to enter in through His Son, Jesus Christ, the captain of the "SS Salvation." Who will listen this time? Many more, I trust. But, again, millions are laughing at God's present-day Noahs.

TOMORROW'S PAPER

Let's breeze through a few present clues that may help us see how close time has skidded to the edge and therefore rejoice at the nearness of golden Millennium!

The Genius Club: The membership of the Club of Rome consists of some of the world's distinguished thinkers and experts from many fields. Recently the C.O.R. undertook a penetrating study of mankind's odds for survival in view of five global threats: runaway population, environmental poisoning, and depletion of energy, raw materials, and food. After inserting all exponential growth data on these into a computer, the C.O.R. experts concluded that earth simply couldn't support its projected life in the near future. It shook the Genius Club!

Zero Population Growth: There are new, unprecedented trends in humanity. Could the recent slowdown in baby production be another edge-of-time indicator? In the 6,000 years since God said, **Be fruitful, and multiply** (Genesis 9:1), there has been an acceleration of births. But now, many first-world nations are approaching zero population growth. Statisticians say that within a matter of years there will be only one child to every four adults. Could this reduction in the number of babies be related to future world carnage? Innocent children would suffer horribly in the coming Armageddon. It's a thought. **Prove all things; hold fast that which is good** (1 Thessalonians 5:21).

Convulsive Crises: Economist Robert Heilbroner wrote an outstanding book entitled *An Inquiry Into the Human Prospect.* He writes,

> The outlook for man is painful, difficult, perhaps desperate.... The answer to whether we can conceive of the future other than as a continuation of the darkness, cruelty, and disorder of the past, seems to me to be no.

Heilbroner sees insurmountable threats to human survival: Runaway population, obliterative war, plus exhaustion of the environment. He believes the only curb in sight to be the Malthusian crises of famine and disease. He sees another disturbing prospect:

> An approaching danger of underdeveloped countries [is] shaking newly obtained atomic bombs in nuclear blackmail to secure massive redistribution of the world's wealth. We now face convulsive change,

forced upon us by breakdown and catastrophe
wherein future survival is at stake and may be possible only under some supergovernment capable of
rallying obedience far more effectively than would be
possible in a democratic setting.

Is the stage being set for a "supergovernment" to be headed
by a brilliant world leader? Will he be the Antichrist?

Paul-Henri Spaak, former prime minister of Belgium and
a leader of the Council of Europe, once issued a statement
that further amplified the world's cries for some superstates-
man to surface.

We do not want another committee. We have too
many already. What we want is a man of sufficient
stature to hold the allegiance of all people, and to lift
us out of the economic morass in which we are
sinking. Send us such a man and, *be he god or the
devil,* we will receive him.

The Bible prophesies that Antichrist will surface, and he will
fit Spaak's description above perfectly!

THE EDGE

Dr. Arnold Toynbee, an eminent British historian and
philosopher, said, "The world now stands on the edge of an
abyss. I see little prospect of humanity righting itself to avoid
some kind of a cataclysmic crash."

Dr. Billy Graham says, "The world is now facing a crisis of such proportions that our whole civilization is threatened."

For we know that the whole creation groaneth and travaileth in pain together until now. Romans 8:22

On a smaller scale, humanity is now functioning with but a thin veneer of decency. People no longer blush at even the grossest sin. The world seems poised in expectancy of new troubles.

Yes, our world is groaning for rescue—holding its breath for some momentous happening. There is great restlessness and a jockeying for power among the nations of the world. Israel and the oil-rich Middle East still perform an especially macabre dance about the world's power button.

Managing the affairs between the nations has become a virtual impossibility. Every institution created to promote international harmony has flopped. The frustrating impotency of the United Nations in the Balkans underscores the failure of man's best efforts. In the last days it is said that there will be distress and perplexities of nations. (See Luke 21:25.)

Angry masses all around the globe are highly ignitable! They seem itching to fight, to steal, and to destroy. "Ethnic cleansing" has entered the language as a euphemism for murdering or driving out every member of a powerless minority. Incendiary speeches of the revolutionaries and the terrorists incite violence and war. The concerted efforts of the evil prince of this world catapult our planet into its death throes.

The thoughts of the late Chairman Mao Zedong inspire the violent slogan, "Power grows out of the barrel of a gun!" Those kidnapped by terrorists and thugs incur millions in ransom. New political kidnappings break out everywhere like some dark plague.

Brutality, terror, and murder stalk the peoples of every nation. In California a long list has been found naming people marked for death or kidnapping by terrorist groups. School children take revenge on their tormentors with automatic weapons. No wonder the Bible said that in the last days, men's hearts would fail them for fear.

A recent newspaper editorial revealed a direct correlation between alcohol consumption and the crisis climate. Breweries and drug peddlers are having a field day selling their reality-blurring potions to sinners who are trying to escape the consequences of their lives.

THE PALE HORSE

Some years ago British author C. P. Snow wrote,

> Perhaps in ten years, millions of people in the poor countries are going to starve to death before our eyes.... We shall see them doing so upon our television sets. But how soon? How many? These are the most important questions in our world today.

When Snow sounded this apocalyptic warning, his hearers dismissed it as unduly alarmist. But Americans have been shocked and dismayed as TV cameras have panned across refugee camps in Rwanda, Sudan, and Uganda, showing thousands of hollow-eyed, bloated, and starving people. God's Book foretold famine galloping through the earth:

> *And I looked, and behold a pale horse: and his name*
> *that sat on him was Death, and Hell followed with him.*
> *And power was given unto them over the fourth part*
> *of the earth, to kill with sword, and with hunger, and*
> *with death, and with the beasts of the earth.* Revelation 6:8

Planet earth has put up with so much from us. Rather than being good stewards of the earth, we have polluted it, sucked its treasures dry, and abused it in ten thousand ways. It has nourished its billions of heaven-defying passengers, but a time of reckoning quickly approaches. Earth needs and will soon get its Millennium respite. Even 2,000 years ago Paul could hear the clock ticking:

> *The night is far spent, the day is at hand:*
> *let us therefore cast off the works of darkness,*
> *and let us put on the armour of light.* Romans 13:12

Present realities depress the drifting masses of today. But to each believer, they are Bible prophecies tolling an end to world corruption and joyously ringing in that rapturous day! Good news is in the wind!

> *For the Lord himself shall descend from heaven with*
> *a shout, with the voice of the archangel, and with the*
> *trump of God: and the dead in Christ shall rise first:*

Then we which are alive and remain shall be caught up together with them in the clouds, to meet the Lord in the air: and so shall we ever be with the Lord. 1 Thessalonians 4:16-17

CHAPTER 5

HAPPINESS IS...

Throughout our present life, flashes of pure joy are like rare diamonds, experienced only rarely and briefly: hearing the first bird of spring, walking hand-in-hand with the one you love, seeing a perfect sunset, or watching kids on Christmas morning.

Life in the end times is no picnic. Too often we find ourselves trudging through days strewn with problems. Sometimes it's cause for celebration just to make it through another week. The carefree times are too infrequent, and joy is hard to find. Why? It's like a woman having labor pains—time is groaning to give birth to a magnificent Millennium:

> *For the anxious longing of the creation waits*
> *eagerly for the revealing of the sons of God.*
> *For we know that the whole creation groans and suffers*
> *the pains of childbirth together until now.* Romans 8:19-22 NASB

Time is a brutal taskmaster. Living by the sweat of the brow is a drag. Little wonder the fearful masses blur their lives with booze and drugs. Pep pills to wake them up, tranquilizers to float them through the day, sleeping pills to knock them out at night. Many people's lives are such tough propositions that they give up. Twentieth-century man feverishly works at the pursuit of happiness but often ends up with only a hangover. Plastic happiness makes big business, while true happiness eludes their grasp.

For believers, it's just the opposite. Happiness pursues them! And in the end, happiness will win out, because the hounds of heaven run more swiftly than the hounds of hell. The warm breezes of the Millennium are about to fill the earth. What a day!

Satan fouled Eden and gained temporary dominion over earth. Since then mankind has struggled in an evil world. Never having experienced anything else, we find it difficult to imagine the exhilaration we're about to feel as all this changes. The moment Satan's evil shorts out, streams of laughter and deep joy will follow. Beauty for ashes—perhaps those incandescent sunsets have been trying to whisper this secret.

Those nagging feelings of restlessness will vanish. Heretofore we have sensed dissatisfaction even during moments of highest pleasure. An indefinable *something* is always missing. That long-awaited vacation, the anticipated moment of bliss, seems *almost* perfect, but never quite is. Do you know what I mean? We will remain incomplete until we are with *Him*. It's Jesus Who will bring forth the *full* spectrum of life, and He's coming soon!

We've been living constantly with pressures and worries, and it will remain that way until Satan is clobbered. He is the father of anxiety, guilt, loneliness, fear, jealousy, nervousness, hopelessness, pain, disappointment, sadness, and hate. But these devastating powers will very soon be brushed into oblivion. The broom of Jesus will sweep them into hell, along with their inventor. Can you stand that kind of a change?

Will you miss the bill collectors? The hourly reports from Bad News Broadcasting Company? The pain of cancer? The surgeon's knife? The bloody wars? Will you miss the lying politicians, the illness, the fat, the funerals? It will take a lot of getting used to, but I think we can make the adjustment! We'd better get ready to live in a brand new kind of world, a world that God has designed on His heavenly drafting board just for us.

So hang tough. We've almost got it made. Let's not falter when we're about to break out of this wearying 6,000-year battle into a dazzling Millennium world. All those things that wear us to a frazzle are just about over. I pray that the reality of the Millennium will so explode in you that the cares of this present time will pale in comparison, and that discouragement can never again take root. Only a God kind of truth has that explosive capacity!

We are nearing a renaissance of Eden's perfection. The restoration of the Garden of Eden begins immediately following Armageddon's fury. How good to be on the inside, knowing we are in a fixed fight and our side wins! Every believer has a

stake in that Armageddon victory and will reap full benefits from this cosmic victory for a thousand years!

When the last doomsday bullet falls back to earth, the curtain will be drawn on this age! Millennial life's hallmarks will be laughter, contentment, purpose, exhilaration, righteousness, peace, ecstasy, and explosive joy! But I must warn you: the true and exotic nature of millennial life might well be labeled "HANDLE WITH CARE." We have to remember that it's Jesus' presence on our planet that will light, power, and beautify the Millennium.

We must check our hearts that it's Jesus we seek and not a new age. Yes, we must handle it with care lest we long for its benefits more than its Benefactor. The real focus of the Millennium will be (and must ever be) the person of Jesus, not the place itself. Jesus is the Millennium's architect, its centerpiece, its all....

Seek ye first the kingdom of God, and his righteousness; and all these things shall be added unto you. Matthew 6:33

CHAPTER 6

GLOBAL URBAN RENEWAL

For years our cities have been the sites of massive urban renewal projects. Have you ever watched the renewal process? First the wrecking crews come. Swarms of bulldozers, wrecking balls and dynamite reduce old, decaying structures to rubble. Then along come the builders who seem to magically erect handsome new facilities. Presto! The area is reborn and made new again.

So it will be with this tired and abused planet. Physical earth also needs to be reborn. But before that happens, I believe everything decadent must be cleared away. Our all-wise, heavenly Father will "plow up the earth" and root out and eliminate everything that won't harmonize with His millennial-life blueprint.

First of all, during the tribulation period God will redistribute the waters and the lands—all within days through earthquakes.

*And there were voices, and thunders, and
lightnings; and there was a great earthquake....
And every island fled away, and the
mountains were not found.* Revelation 16:18, 20

God will also cause great rearrangements of the firmament
that will both enhance the cosmetics of the planet and provide
vast, new habitable land area. Earth presently has an enormous
140 million-square-mile land area hiding under its oceans.
These future land masses include mountains higher than Mt.
Everest and chasms deeper than the Grand Canyon—realms
to provide the most pleasant scenery. All present faults and
strains in the earth's crust will be relieved during that series of
explosive quakes, and when the dust settles, our planet will be
entirely earthquake-free.

*Behold, the Lord maketh the earth empty, and
maketh it waste, and turneth it upside down,
and scattereth abroad the inhabitants thereof....
And it will fall, and not rise again.* Isaiah 24:1, 20

The finger of God may also correct the 22-degree tilt of the
earth on its axis and its periodic wobble at the same time.
These may have been caused by the violence in Lucifer's rebellion. Meteorologists say these irregularities contribute to the
climate extremes: hurricanes, floods, blizzards, droughts, and
other natural disasters. With her tilt and wobble corrected, we
will see an idealizing of earth's climate. God says,

And I will cause the shower to come down
in his season; there shall be showers of blessing.
And the tree of the field shall yield her fruit. Ezekiel 34:26-27

Through the prophet Isaiah we are told,

The parched ground shall become a pool, and the thirsty land
springs of water: in the habitation of dragons, where each lay,
shall be grass with reeds and rushes. Isaiah 35:7

DAY OF THE ROGUES

Renewal won't take place just in earth's geography. It is my
believe that earth's *spiritual* geography will be revamped:

The Son of man shall send forth his angels,
and they shall gather out of his kingdom all things
that offend, and them which do iniquity. Matthew 13:41

When I used to think of these years of chaos, my suspicious
mind visualized a random annihilation of the people unfortunate
enough to be alive. But God will see that the angels exercise
great care in this vital end-time sorting. They will be under
very tight rein. (See Matthew 13.) There is nothing "chancy"
in God's character.

Often through history, God has moved under a divine principle of screening out the righteous before a great judgment
begins. We see this with Noah's family before the flood and
with Lot's family before the destruction of Sodom.

Another such time involved Ezekiel whom the Spirit lifted up between the earth and the heaven. While there he was shown a vision of this godly principle in action. Ezekiel saw that the city of Jerusalem had become the scene of many abominations. God described it as **the land full of blood and the city full of perverseness** (Ezekiel 9:9). Because of this wickedness, the Lord called out six men with weapons and one man with a writer's inkhorn. He said to the man with the inkhorn,

> *Go through the midst of the city, through the midst of Jerusalem, and set a mark upon the foreheads of the men that sigh and that cry for all the abominations that be done in the midst thereof. Ezekiel 9:4*

After the mark of God had been placed on the forehead of each person who hated unrighteousness, a final order was given to the slayers:

> *Slay utterly old and young, both maids, and little children, and women: but come not near any man upon whom is the mark; and begin at my sanctuary. Ezekiel 9:6*

It is sobering that God started with the church people. He always deals with those of His own household first.

QUALITY CONTROL

God will carefully read the heart of each person during those last-chance tribulation years. Those He sees who have the potential to harmonize with the upcoming reign of Jesus will

be spared. God's longing for all to be spared can be seen in
His Word:

> *Say unto them, As I live, saith the Lord God,*
> *I have no pleasure in the death of the wicked; but that*
> *the wicked turn from his way and live: turn ye, turn ye*
> *from your evil ways; for why will ye die. Ezekiel 33:11*

Those who turn to the living God will gain favor and salvation.

> *And a book of remembrance was written before him for*
> *them that feared the Lord, and that thought upon his name.*
> *And they shall be mine, saith the Lord of hosts,*
> *in that day when I make up my jewels;*
> *and I will spare them. Malachi 3:16-17*

But all the rest, those who irreversibly harden their heart
toward God, must be screened out. Many will have given
themselves over to lasciviousness, rebellion, and violence. They
will be irretrievable. These will be marked as "rogue humans."
They probably wouldn't like Millennium life or heaven either,
for that matter. Hell will better suit their style since, of their
own accord, they will have chosen against God.

God is never whimsical; His sorting of humanity will be
scathingly accurate, absolutely just and lovingly deliberate.

> *And he shall separate them one from another,*
> *as a shepherd divideth his sheep from the goats....*

Then shall the King say unto them on his right hand,
Come, ye blessed of my Father, inherit the kingdom prepared for
you from the foundation of the world. Matthew 25:32,34

God's inspection plan bears the cutting edge of truth, doesn't it? A loving heavenly Father will separate for Himself a people who can blend with one another throughout the 1,000-year reign of Jesus on earth.

MILLENNIUM RESTORATION

Millennial life will be an era of great purpose; a season when the work of earth's rehabilitation must be accomplished. First Armageddon, then to work! There will be limited time for "harping," praise God! Earth will be plowed and ready for our loving attention, ready to be replanted, rebuilt, and reorganized.

Modern Israel depicts a striking type of the restoration work that must take place in the earth during the Millennium. The Lord granted Abraham a title in perpetuity to the territory that includes present-day Israel. After centuries of putting up with Jewish defiance, God temporarily drove them from their own land. During their absence, and while under alien steward-ship, the land grew barren and desolate. Stripped of trees, untilled, and unwatered, the Promised Land became wasteland. Finally, the Jews were able to return from the Diaspora to their devastated inheritance.

Now Israel is being restored. In a dramatic fulfillment of prophecy, the Jews are being gathered from the four corners of the world into Israel. Similarly the Bible tells how, at the close of Armageddon, the Jews and all righteous Gentiles will again be gathered up under God's direction. The Bible foretold how, under God's blessing, *and by the work of their own hands,* the Jews would so transform the land that visitors would exclaim, "It looks like the Garden of Eden!" This has come to pass in our day. (See Ezekiel 36:35.)

In contrast, the millennial rebuilding will be accomplished through both supernatural acts and by human endeavor. We can look forward to witnessing all the changes in this exquisite planet while it is being progressively restored to its Edenic perfection.

Millennium citizenry will include all of the saints, plus the remaining few millions of unsaved people still alive at the conclusion of Armageddon. As King of the earth, Jesus will lead and direct the entire society from Jerusalem, the world's capital. He will delegate authority and power to the saints who will reign over designated areas under Him as He did in the following parable:

> *And he said unto him, Well* [done], *thou good servant: because thou hast been faithful in a very little, have thou authority over ten cities. Luke 19:17*

The Millennium won't mean the inauguration of a classless society, but one with well-defined orders, allowing a high order of efficiency under our Lord's direction.

Are you exhausted already just thinking about your assignments during the Millennium? Well, during that glorious time, it will never be tiring for believers. It will be a stimulating time because we will experience the vitality of immortality pulsing in every cell. Our knowledge, wisdom, and ability will have been instantly expanded at the moment of our resurrection. We will have the mind of Christ. Never again will we experience brain fade, mental sluggishness, or forgetfulness. The dynamic of resurrection power will be ours at last. Complex problems will then become very simple. Assignments will be easy for us. The joyful sounds of progress will grace the Millennium years.

David's description in Psalm 18 gives us a good idea of just how awesome Jesus' presence will be on earth during the Millennium:

> The Lord descended from above,
> And bowed the heavens most high,
> And underneath His feet He cast
> The darkness of the sky.
> On cherubim and seraphim
>
> Full royally He rode,
> And on the wings of mighty winds
> Came flying all abroad.
>
> He sat serene upon the floods,
> Their fury to restrain;
> And He, as sovereign Lord and King,
> For evermore shall reign.
>
> —Psalm 18 paraphrase by Thomas Sternhold, 1587

What a day!

CHAPTER 7

THE PLACE TO BE

In the last chapter we discussed how earth's physical and spiritual geography will be altered for the Millennium, but earth's political and social geography will also undergo radical changes. For example, Jerusalem will be the all-purpose capital of the world by then. (See Revelation 21 and Zechariah 14.)

Conveniently located between Jerusalem and the sprawling city of Tel Aviv, Israel's Ben-Gurion Airport is big! Ben-Gurion has a complex of runways and facilities that enable it to handle most of Israel's commercial and military air traffic. In the coming age, however, this great airport won't be able to handle even a fraction of the global visitors. Into her will stream multitudes of joyous people by the airways, sea lanes, and highways.

Millennial Jerusalem will become a very big city. The prophetic scriptures speak of vast numbers of people coming up to the city:

And it shall come to pass in the last days,
that the mountain of the Lord's house shall be
established in the top of the mountains, and shall be exalted
above the hills; and all nations shall flow unto it. Isaiah 2:2

That scripture also implies that the mountains on which millennial Jerusalem will sit will become even higher, possibly due to the great earthquake that occurs on the Mount of Olives when Jesus returns. At the same time, Jerusalem will also become a riverside city. The very moment Jesus steps onto the Mount of Olives, the mountain will split and a magnificent new river will flow out in either direction:

And his feet shall stand in that day upon the mount of Olives,
which is before Jerusalem on the east, and the mount of Olives
shall cleave in the midst thereof toward the east and toward
the west, and there shall be a very great valley; and half
of the mountain shall remove toward the north,
and half of it toward the south.
And it shall be in that day, that living waters shall go out
from Jerusalem; half of them toward the former sea,
and half of them toward the hinder sea. Zechariah 14:4,8

From the Talmud we catch a hint of the dazzling beauty of the millennial city: "Ten parts of beauty were allotted the world at large; out of these Jerusalem assumed nine measures and the rest of the world but one." Looking through prophetic eyes toward millennial Jerusalem, Jeremiah wrote,

Therefore they shall come and sing in the height of Zion, and shall flow together to the goodness of the Lord. Jeremiah 31:12

And Isaiah, who seems to sing his inspired view of the jubilant influx, wrote,

Therefore the redeemed of the Lord shall return, and come with singing unto Zion; and everlasting joy shall be upon their head: they shall obtain gladness and joy; and sorrow and mourning shall flee away. Isaiah 51:11

In that day, Jerusalem will be *The Place* to go. God says,

And I will pour upon the house of David, and upon the inhabitants of Jerusalem, the spirit of grace and of supplications. Zechariah 12:10

World action will be centered in Jerusalem, and each year it will be our privilege to visit that City of Blessings:

And I will make them and the places round about my hill a blessing; and I will cause the shower to come down in his season; there shall be showers of blessing. Ezekiel 34:26

There's an interesting aspect to those yearly trips to Jerusalem during the kingdom era. Although traffic in and out of the Holy City will be enormous, Jesus will keep track of anyone who neglects to come. He will strongly desire that each person visit Jerusalem every year, and there is going to be a little penalty for shirkers:

> *And it shall come to pass, that every one that is left*
> *of all the nations which came against Jerusalem shall*
> *even go up from year to year to worship the King,*
> *the Lord of hosts, and to keep the feast of tabernacles.*
> *And it shall be, that whoso will not come up of all the families*
> *of the earth unto Jerusalem to worship the King, the Lord of*
> *hosts, even upon them* shall be no rain. *Zechariah 14:16-17*

All manner of people will flow into the beautiful city. Some will be coming to worship at the great millennial temple that Jesus himself will build.

> *Even he shall build the temple of the Lord; and he shall*
> *bear the glory, and shall sit and rule upon his throne;*
> *and he shall be a priest upon his throne.* *Zechariah 6:13*

Then again we hear of this same new temple, through the prophet Ezekiel:

> *My sanctuary shall be in the midst*
> *of them for evermore.* *Ezekiel 37:28*

Others in the stream of Jerusalem-bound travelers will be coming to transact administrative affairs of the new worldwide government. It will be a very efficient administration with believers holding all the key posts.

*They shall be priests of God and of Christ, and
shall reign with him a thousand years.* Revelation 20:6

*And he that overcometh, and keepeth my works unto
the end, to him will I give power over the nations:
And he shall rule them.* Revelation 2:26-27

Although we will rule and reign with Jesus Christ in the
Millennium, He will be the supreme political and spiritual
leader of the whole world:

*And the Lord shall be king over all the earth:
in that day shall there be one Lord.* Zechariah 14:9

This era will see an end of society's fragmentation because
of diverse religions, languages, regimes, and political systems.

LAW AND ORDER

We are in a frightening hour when justice is mocked. Many
judges are weak and our courts are a shambles. Too frequently
the guilty rich go unpunished while the poor suffer. The court
calendars are so glutted that justice has become slow and
frighteningly uncertain. Truth has become elastic and, as a
consequence, our civilization is reeling.

Millennial justice, on the other hand, will blend wisdom,
authority, and fairness as never before experienced in the earth.
Isaiah saw this aspect of Jesus' rule:

Of the increase of his government and peace
there shall be no end, upon the throne of David,
and upon his kingdom, to order it, and to
establish it with judgment and with justice. Isaiah 9:7

All the things we long for in government Jesus will supply. Again through Isaiah we read of this dispensing of pure justice:

He shall bring forth judgment unto truth.
He shall not fail nor be discouraged,
till he have set judgment in the earth: and
the isles shall wait for his law. Isaiah 42:3-4

No one will get away with anything! And Jesus' rule will also banish earth's bloody warring.

And he shall judge among the nations, and shall rebuke
many people: and they shall beat their swords into
plowshares, and their spears into pruninghooks:
nation shall not lift up sword against nation,
neither shall they learn war any more. Isaiah 2:4

What's more, Jerusalem will also become a fun city in the finest sense:

The voice of joy, and the voice of gladness, the voice of
the bridegroom, and the voice of the bride, the voice of them
that shall say, Praise the Lord of hosts. Jeremiah 33:11

Yes, in the perpetual presence of her Bridegroom, millennial Jerusalem will ring with laughter, excitement, dancing, and purpose. It will be electrifying just to enter her gates!

CAMPUS NEWS

Some of the visitors to Jerusalem will be coming as students to study at "Jesus University."

> *...Let us go up to the mountain of the Lord...*
> *and he will teach us of his ways.*   Micah 4:2

Isaiah wrote of those mind-enriching courses:

> **And all thy children shall be**
> **taught of the Lord.** Isaiah 54:13

Can you picture us strolling across the Jerusalem campus of Jesus U heading for our classes? Maybe we'll be taking courses like:

Advanced Planet Management
Secrets of the Universe
Divine Principles
Celestial Music
Animal Stewardship
Universal Laws
Cosmic Energy
Celestial Travel
Galaxy Pioneering

Yes, it could be. I always grumbled about going to school, but I can hardly wait to enroll in those classes where the Lord will be sharing deep secrets with us. By then we will have proven ourselves trustworthy to receive a firsthand unlocking of many of His great mysteries. And because we will be joint heirs and rulers with Jesus for eternity, such knowledge will be essential for us to carry out our designated assignments.

With all this to look forward to, the Lord doesn't want us to coast in our present spiritual state, waiting for millennial classes to learn of His kingdom. We have been exhorted to hit our studies hard while in this present life:

> *Study to shew thyself approved unto God,*
> *a workman that needeth not to be ashamed,*
> *rightly dividing the word of truth.* 2 Timothy 2:15

We should accelerate our intake of the Word in the time left in this age. God reveals still more to those who grow in grace and the knowledge of Him. This is a divine principle. It isn't feasible to take a crash course in the totally unfamiliar. What we know by the time of the Millennium can serve as a bridge over which to discover further treasures now hidden in God!

While the Millennium will provide an incredible post-graduate course in the spiritual world, the undergraduate courses are going on now as you ground yourself thoroughly in God's Word. Don't drop out, and don't drop back to kindergarten. Study to show yourself approved unto God so you'll hear that heart-expanding greeting at the kingdom gate:

> *Well done, thou good and faithful servant...*
> *enter thou into the joy of thy lord.* Matthew 25:21

CHAPTER 8

THE TIME MACHINE

Armageddon, that great battle which takes place in Israel prior to the Millennium, will be a terrible slaughter of armies. To prevent total annihilation, Jesus will, at the peak of Armageddon's fury, smite the bow and arrows out of the hand of His enemies. Their guns will be spiked and the Antichrist and the False Prophet thrown into the lake of fire. (See Revelation 20.) Satan will be forcibly chained and imprisoned.

Immediately following the lock-up ceremony, I believe that every earthling who has survived Armageddon will go through a moral and spiritual "x-raying." There will be no hiding place in all the world for the fleeing wicked. This all takes place during a day of strange twilight:

> *And it shall come to pass in that day,*
> *that the light shall not be clear, nor dark:*

But it shall come to pass, that at evening
time it shall be light. Zechariah 14:6-7

I believe Scripture tells us that mighty angels will track the wicked to their most remote hideouts. Every single person who is spiritually incurable will be denied entrance to the Millennium. The Lord will block evil, corrupt humans from infecting or tormenting believers in the new age.

Reprobates will have sealed their own fate by resisting Jesus Christ's salvation during this lifetime. Scripture points to this decision on their part:

Men loved darkness rather than light,
because their deeds were evil. John 3:19

Who knowing the judgment of God, that they which commit
such things are worthy of death, not only do the same,
but have pleasure in them that do them. Romans 1:32

Their sick joke, "Yeah, Jesus saves—*trading stamps!*" will burn in many ears for eternity.

The Bible gives us precedents for the divine elimination of hopeless incorrigibles: The priests of Baal were destroyed on Mount Carmel for contending with God's prophet, Elijah. Corrupted Sodomites were dispatched in one blinding flash! *Attention, homosexuals and lesbians!* Don't fall for the lie that God has suddenly changed His mind and will lovingly accept your sinful lifestyle. It won't happen.

As I mentioned before, Ezekiel plainly saw God's repulsion toward unrighteousness in a prophetic vision when God ordered the man with an inkhorn to **set a mark upon the foreheads of the men that sign and that cry for all the abominations that be done in the midst thereof** (Ezekiel 9:4). Immediately after God's man had duly marked all the righteous people, He spoke again. This time six slayers were given their orders.

> *And to the others* (the unrighteous) *he said in mine hearing, Go ye after him through the city, and smite: let not your eye spare, neither have ye pity: Slay utterly...but come not near any man upon whom is the mark; and begin at my sanctuary.* Ezekiel 9:5-6

God's attitude toward evil, so starkly outlined in that vision, may at first seem harsh. But instead, it reveals what He *must do* to prevent the wicked from again corrupting millennial civilization. And don't think that being a good church member will cover you! God's post-Armageddon inspection will start with the Church—with a spiritual "x-raying" of His own household first.

There is another account in the New Testament which reveals the shock of certain persons who, when they approached the kingdom of heaven, were told by Jesus,

> *I never knew you: depart from me, ye that work iniquity.* Matthew 7:23

The only key that will work the golden tumblers of heaven's lock is righteousness through Jesus Christ. Why, of course! How could a holy God spend an eternity with the unrighteous, even though they had done mighty works in the sight of men? In that passage they had futilely sputtered,

> *Lord, Lord, have we not prophesied in thy name?...and in thy name done many wonderful works?* Matthew 7:22

The day fast approaches when each of us must walk through heaven's door! Do you have that one and only key? Hurry, there's still time to get it!

Today we hear so much "God is love" talk. Ignoring biblical evidence to the contrary, many people, Christians and non-Christians, really believe that "a God of love wouldn't really send me to hell, would He?" Sure, He's a God of love, but it's essential to remember He's also a God of *justice.* Since He's a God of love, He sent us Jesus to die for our sins and therefore satisfy His justice. If we don't accept that sacrificial death, we must pay the price for our sins ourselves.

No plastic, counterfeit religionists will make it through heaven's door based on their own idea of God. Jesus is the only way. Jesus accurately said,

> *I am the way, the truth, and the life: no man cometh unto the Father, but by me.* John 14:6

The Jesus-key is the only one that can ever gain access to the Father.

THY KINGDOM COME

Once we're through the millennial gate, we'll have no more nightmares, insomnia, anxiety, confusion, disappointment, or fear. No longer will that old false accuser cause painful memory flashbacks. God will erase harmful memories of those dark events from our past.

God shall wipe away all tears from their eyes. Revelation 7:17

Isn't that great? We couldn't have "joy unspeakable and full of glory" if our sorrowful memories were dragged along into the Millennium.

Then picture all of those *Out of Business* signs on clock factories. I can just hear you saying, "What's that—did you say clock factories?" Yes, I believe there may be a few clock factories around for the benefit of non-glorified people, but the glorified saints will have little need for clocks, watches, or calendars. Perhaps you can sell that Timex stock. We won't have too much use for their little time machines during the kingdom age.

COSMIC SYNCHRONIZATION

One day I was thinking about the implications of a clockless Millennium, and it seemed to me that mass confusion would surely result. Though clocks are terrible little taskmasters, they have become essential to coordinate our civilization.

I hate the pressing nature of time, but even so I really couldn't operate without it. I wondered how could we ever possibly do without our watch during the Millennium? Then the Lord began to show me a few things about time itself. Jesus' name, Alpha and Omega, reveals that He is the originator and perpetuator of time. He has precise awareness of events, progress, and fulfillment. He charts the course and rhythms of the universe. Yet the feeble ticking of man can never pressure Jesus' little time machines.

I said, "But Lord, how could millennial believers ever function without watches? How would we ever keep appointments? Wouldn't there be rank confusion without our clocks?"

He reminded me of a personal episode I had completely forgotten. "Remember that trip when you forgot your travel alarm and you prayed to be awakened at 6:30?"

I said, "Yes, Lord, I do remember! I had been astonished when I turned on the light in my Dallas hotel room to find it was exactly 6:30 A.M.!"

He said, "I answered that prayer by effecting just one of the benefits of the coming age. During this present life, everything on earth suffers from disharmony with the rest of My creation. The rhythms in space, where sin has never touched, are still run with sheer perfection. The finest chronometers mankind has ever built are inadequate to measure the precision of their orbits. Every star and galaxy moves with fine geometric grace. Do I ever bring the sun up late?

"Clocks serve mankind as a temporary crutch. They are essential while nature is in disarray through sin, out of synchronization with the rest of My universe. In the instant of the believer's resurrection, every scar from the curse will be healed. You will then find yourself in perfect harmony with all creation. Suddenly you will know what time it is! Everyone has experienced instances of sensing the correct time without the benefit of a clock. When you put on immortality, this quality will be perfected in you. Then you will always know exactly what time it is."

Why, of course, for then we will know as Jesus knows. No one can picture Jesus peering at a wristwatch! And so it will be no problem to function most efficiently in the coming age without those pesky clocks. We will then know what to do and when to do it through our new oneness with Him. This divine internal clock will enhance the silky smoothness and harmony of society in the Millennium. Internal clocks are just one more way God fulfills His Word:

> *That in the ages to come he might show*
> *the exceeding riches of his grace in his kindness*
> *toward us through Christ Jesus.* *Ephesians 2:7*

Chapter 9

Falling Lightning!

And I saw an angel come down from heaven, having the
key of the bottomless pit and a great chain in his hand.
And he laid hold on the dragon, that old serpent, which is
the Devil, and Satan, and bound him a thousand years,
And cast him into the bottomless pit, and shut him up, and
set a seal upon him, that he should deceive the nations no
more, till the thousand years should be fulfilled. Revelation 20:1-3

What a relief! On the day Satan is bound, the planet's atmosphere will experience a sudden switch in polarity—from negative to positive! The generators of hell will be switched off! Those satanic forces we have struggled with for so long will simply disappear. No more will Satan fan our impulses of lust, anger, fear, or hate.

Holiness will be the Millennium's hallmark. Those with a tendency toward sin and rebellion will be constrained. Why? Jesus will be in charge:

*And a King shall reign and prosper, and shall
execute judgment and justice in the earth.* Jeremiah 23:5

In the coming Satan-free world, God's discipline will still be required among the non-glorified citizenry to avoid spiritual failure. Even without help from Satan, they will still have to contend with that potential for evil within themselves.

Does this mean their sinning will darken millennial life? Although there will be sin among the non-glorified during the Millennium, it will be minimal. Righteousness will dominate for these reasons: 1) Satan will be chained, 2) there will be a holy environment, 3) millennial society will be governed with a firm hand, and 4) Jesus will be in residence on the planet.

But, amazingly, toward the end of God's 1,000-year display of near-idyllic life, trouble looms again. The Scriptures say,

*And when the thousand years are expired,
Satan shall be loosed out of his prison,
And shall go out to deceive the nations which are in the
four quarters of the earth, Gog and Magog, to gather them
together to battle: the number of whom is as the sand of the sea.
And they went up on the breadth of the earth,
and compassed the camp of the saints about,
and the beloved city.* Revelation 20:7-9

You say, "Good grief! Not again!" Yes, somehow Satan is able to recruit a big army from among the millennial masses. They march to attack the saints in Jerusalem. Non-glorified citizens who have secretly carried a yearning for sin begin to polarize around that magnet of evil. Satan concludes his final work by exposing these evil-prone people. In the end, the army of the wicked is destroyed. The rest of that passage says:

And fire came down from God
out of heaven, and devoured them.
And the devil that deceived them was cast into
the lake of fire and brimstone, where the beast
and the false prophet are, and shall be tormented
day and night for ever and ever. Revelation 20:9-10

Satan joins the Antichrist and the False Prophet, who have been waiting for him in the lake of fire since Armageddon. Pride-choked Lucifer reaches his eternal address. God always has the final word!

PASSPORT DENIED

As we see the big picture, it becomes clear that no sin/fun in this life is worth jeopardizing our passports to that Jesus-empowered Millennium. We should be **choosing rather to suffer affliction with the people of God, than to enjoy the pleasures of sin for a season** (Hebrews 11:25). May our Millennium credentials never be stamped, *"Passport Denied,"* because of our failure to recognize God's attitude about holy living through Christ. May we remember those chilling words spoken to the ungodly:

...neither fornicators, nor idolaters, nor adulterers,
nor effeminate, nor abusers of themselves with mankind,
Nor thieves, nor covetous, nor drunkards,
nor revilers, nor extortioners, shall inherit
the kingdom of God. 1 Corinthians 6:9-10

The Church has recently emphasized liberty in the Christian life, but *liberty* has too often skidded over into *license*. Too many believers are drifting into traps of situational ethics and situational spirituality. In this hour, so near time's edge, it's intelligent to walk the line, to keep our focus on the Lord, and to let His Word and His Spirit rule our hearts and minds.

Be ye also patient; stablish your hearts:
for the coming of the Lord draweth nigh. James 5:8

Chapter 10

Secret of the Indestructibles

Listen now to God's covenant promise for His chosen people!

Therefore they shall come and sing in the height of Zion,
and shall flow together to the goodness of the Lord,
for wheat, and for wine, and for oil, and for the young
of the flock and of the herd: and their soul shall be as a
watered garden; and they shall not sorrow any more at all.
Then shall the virgin rejoice in the dance, both young
men and old together: for I will turn their mourning
into joy, and will comfort them. Jeremiah 31:12-13

Is this just melodic poetry, or is it an actual and electrifying preview of a soon-coming event? It's for real, all right. It is God's covenant promise of blessing to the Jews—one of those exquisite prophetic scriptures with a dual fulfillment. Jeremiah not only foresaw the Jews' entrance into the Promised Land, but he also caught God's longer-range view of upcoming millennial delights. It's as certain to happen as tomorrow morning's sunrise!

Even though the Jews have often grieved God, His love for them is unquenchable:

For the Lord shall comfort Zion: he will comfort all her waste places; and he will make her wilderness like Eden, and her desert like the garden of the Lord; joy and gladness shall be found therein, thanksgiving, and the voice of melody. Isaiah 51:3

The Bible is interlaced with rich millennial commitments for His chosen people. Even so, certain wicked Jews must first be weeded out:

For they are not all Israel, which are of Israel. Romans 9:6

But what a celebration is coming for every Jew who, during the Tribulation, will resist the Antichrist's seduction! On the day of Jesus Christ's return, every Jew will instantly recognize Him as Messiah:

They shall know me, from the least of them unto the greatest of them, saith the Lord: for I will forgive their iniquity, and I will remember their sin no more. Jeremiah 31:34

For so long the Jews have taken bitter persecution for being known as the people of God. But soon full compensation will come to them for all that persecution! Since Israel fully liberated Jerusalem in the Six-Day War of 1967, we have seen a growing phenomenon: Multiplying signs of the "budding of the fig tree" which Jesus said would indicate that "summer is nigh." Jews from Ethiopia and the former Soviet Union are making *aliya* by the thousands, returning to the Promised Land. What's more, thousands of Jews are discovering the truth that Yeshua (Jesus) is indeed their Messiah. The Lord has begun to fulfill His promise to lift the spiritual slumber of the Jews. It's happening today and it will steadily increase.

Behold, I will bring them from the north country, and gather them from the coasts of the earth, and with them the blind and the lame, the woman with child and her that travaileth with child together: a great company shall return thither.

They shall come with weeping, and with supplications will I lead them: I will cause them to walk by the rivers of waters in a straight way, wherein they shall not stumble: for I am a father to Israel, and Ephraim is my firstborn.

Hear the word of the Lord, O ye nations, and declare it in the isles afar off, and say, He that scattered Israel will gather him, and keep him, as a shepherd doth his flock.

For the Lord hath redeemed Jacob, and ransomed him from the hand of him that was stronger than he. Jeremiah 31:8-11

Right in the midst of the Antichrist's Tribulation reign, a great Jewish revival will break out. The Bible tells about the remarkable 144,000 witnesses. (See Revelation 7:4.) Through the Antichrist's persecutions, the Jews will be readied to receive Yeshua Ha Mashiach (Jesus the Messiah) at last. Through the prophet Hosea, God foretold,

I will go and return to my place, till they acknowledge
their offense, and seek my face: in their affliction
they will seek me early. Hosea 5:15

By the time Jesus comes back with the saints to defeat and
chain Satan, the Jews will be spiritually ripe. A most incredible
event will then take place. The world will see an entire nation
saved in one single day!

And so all Israel shall be saved: as it is written,
There shall come out of Sion the Deliverer, and shall
turn away ungodliness from Jacob. Romans 11:26

Wow! Are you ready for that? God looks forward to that day
with great eagerness:

And I will rejoice in Jerusalem, and joy in my people:
and the voice of weeping shall be no more heard
in her, nor the voice of crying. Isaiah 65:19

Yes, the Jews will come, in spite of their centuries-long rejection of God's Son:

Shall the earth be made to bring forth in one day?
or shall a nation be born at once? for as soon as
Zion travailed, she brought forth her children....
Rejoice ye with Jerusalem, and be
glad with her, all ye that love her....
As one whom his mother comforteth, so will I
comfort you; and you shall be comforted in Jerusalem.

And when ye see this, your heart shall rejoice, and your
bones shall flourish like an herb: and the hand of the Lord
shall be known toward his servants. Isaiah 66:8,10,13-14

Some scholars believe David himself will return in a governing role:

And David my servant shall be king over them. Ezekiel 37:24

Though most Bible students feel this scripture is referring to Jesus, the seed of David, there is another possibility. Surely God's beloved David himself will be among the Millennium saints who will be ruling and reigning in some capacity.

Yes, harvest day is fast approaching for the Jewish indestructibles:

Israel shall be saved in the Lord with
an everlasting salvation. Isaiah 45:17

Jeremiah put it this way:

And they shall teach no more every man his neighbour,
and every man his brother, saying, Know the Lord:
for they shall ALL know me, from the least of them
unto the greatest of them. Jeremiah 31:34

And so, every saint who has been filtered, tried, and spiritually perfected faces a golden future. The redeemed, both Jew and Gentile, will forever live with the Lord.

And the ransomed of the Lord shall return, and
come to Zion with songs and everlasting joy upon
their heads: they shall obtain joy and gladness, and
sorrow and sighing shall flee away. Isaiah 35:10

Seiss' whole being was exercised when he thought about this coming new age:

The earth is now full of ailment and disorders, and in deep captivity to corruption. Yet it still has much attractiveness. Carpeted with green, girded with glorious mountains, ribboned with rivers. But this is only the OLD earth in its soiled and work-a-day garb, where the miseries of a deep, dark and universal apostasy from God holds sway. Think then what its regeneration must bring!

An earth which no longer smarts and smokes under the curse of sin—an earth which needs no more to be torn with hooks and irons to make it yield its fruit—an earth where thorns and thistles no longer infest the ground, nor serpents hiss among the flowers, nor savage beasts lay in ambush to devour—an earth whose sod is never cut with graves, whose soil is never moistened with tears or saturated with human blood.

Whose atmosphere never gives wing to the seeds of plague and death, whose ways are never blocked with armed men on their way to war—an earth that ever glows with salvation, and whose valleys know only the sweetness of God's pleasure—PARADISE RESTORED!

John Walvoord's soul was also shaken as he rejoiced at Israel's role in the looming kingdom age:

> God has promised Israel a glorious future and this
> will be fulfilled after the Second Advent. Israel will
> be a glorious nation, protected from her enemies,
> exalted above the Gentiles, the central vehicle of the
> manifestation of God's grace in the millennial
> kingdom. In the present age, Israel has been set
> aside, her promises held in abeyance....

Yes, the Jews will forever enjoy an intimate compartment in the heart of God. God's special love for them will become very evident to all millennial citizenry.

> *And strangers shall stand and feed your flocks, and the sons*
> *of the alien shall be your plowmen and your vinedressers.*
> *But ye shall be named the Priests of the Lord:*
> *men shall call you the Ministers of our God:*
> *ye shall eat the riches of the Gentiles.... all that*
> *see them shall acknowledge them, that they are*
> *the seed which the Lord hath blessed....*
> *he hath covered me with the robe of righteousness, as a*
> *bridegroom decketh himself with ornaments. Isaiah 61:5-6,9-10*

Our Lord will repay *with high interest* every righteous Jew who has suffered during the centuries of persecution for being known as one of His people. In the new age, a redeemed Jew will be a prized friend—the Bible speaks of this repeatedly:

*In those days it shall come to pass, that ten men shall take
hold out of all languages of the nations, even shall take hold
of the skirt of him that is a Jew, saying, We will go with you:
for we have heard that God is with you.* Zechariah 8:23

*Now if the fall of them be the riches of the world, and
the diminishing of them the riches of the Gentiles;
how much more their fulness?* Romans 11:12

When, long ago, God said He would bless those who bless
the Jews, He was expressing an eternal attitude. So it would be
well to discipline our attitudes concerning God's chosen. It
may stand us well as further preparation for the dawning age.
From the vantage point of eternity, believers will learn just how
much we owe the eternal Jew. We should, accordingly, never be
jealous of their place in God's heart, but rejoice along with
Him over them:

*The Lord thy God hath chosen thee to be a special
people unto himself, above all people that are
upon the face of the earth.* Deuteronomy 7:6

Imagine how Jewish hearts will burn when the full impact of
God's special love becomes fully evident to them! God is even
going to sing love songs to them!

*The Lord thy God in the midst of thee is mighty;
he will save, he will rejoice over thee with joy; he will rest in
his love, he will joy over thee* with singing. *Zephaniah 3:17*

Thank You, God, for the Jews who brought down to us Your Word, Your ways, and Your Son!

> *He shall cause them that come of Jacob to take root:*
> *Israel shall blossom and bud, and fill the*
> *face of the world with fruit.* Isaiah 27:6

CHAPTER 11

THE FRAGRANCE OF GOD

Have you ever noticed the smell and feel of the air during a thunderstorm? The air seems to be electrically charged, and every good, fresh smell seems to be amplified by the storm. The air of the Millennium is going to be mighty exciting—like distilled lightning—and we'll breathe the pure, clear fragrance of God!

It's certainly not like that now. In fact, it stinks. Satan looked like the winner when Jesus hung bloody and lifeless up there on Golgotha. The devil's kingdom must have celebrated wildly, crying "Victory at last!" But their gloating smirks froze when three days later resurrection power bolted through the universe, raising Jesus from the dead. Satan had played his trump card and lost!

Just as Jesus was able to survive Satan's powerful blows, so shall it be with us. Ever since Jesus conquered Satan, we believers have been equipped for triumph in spiritual warfare.

Christians are the gem-like remnant sifted from humanity who have, one by one, chosen to follow the Jesus they have never seen.

We are believers who through this Jesus ran life's gauntlet of temptation, crises, and pain, only to emerge with the prize of immortality. We are like a radiant cluster of stars, ready for presentation to the heavenly Father as proof of redeemable creation—later to be whisked a million light-years away to glittering corners of the universe as a proud display. We're Jesus' victory trophies!

Our hearts will melt when we hear all creation tuned up and praising God in full concert! Would you believe the hills and the trees actually joining our chorus? They will, according to Isaiah 55:12:

> *The mountains and the hills shall break forth*
> *before you into singing, and all the trees*
> *of the field shall clap their hands.*

We can almost see the clear waters, brilliant skies, singing hills, lush greenery, and brilliant Millennium flowers—and no more choking weeds; no devouring insects; no more killing droughts. We will hear the pleasant sounds of progress, and the whole tempo of the universe will become melodic.

> *Let the heavens rejoice, and let the earth be glad;*
> *let the sea roar, and the fulness thereof.*
> *Let the field be joyful, and all that is therein: then*
> *shall all the trees of the wood rejoice. Psalm 96:11-12*

The Millennium will be the ultimate fulfillment of Jesus' prayer:

Our Father which art in heaven, Hallowed be thy name.
Thy kingdom come. Thy will be done
in earth, as it is in heaven. Matthew 6:9-10

Can't you sense its nearness?

Recently, I visited Lakeport, a beautiful lake village in Northern California. In my first meeting I told the gathering about a reaction I had when I first arrived. "Most of you know I live in Los Angeles. During my first hour in Lakeport, I was mystified by a peculiar 'something' in the air. You people are used to it, but a stranger can immediately smell it. I suppose we've all discovered that our own home has a distinctive odor, all its own. We seem to adjust to its smell; never noticing it until we've been gone for a while.

"Some of you have suffered the 'fragrance' of cities like Gary, Indiana; Los Angeles; or Pittsburgh. Or maybe you have suffered from some town with a stockyard upwind. Haven't you wondered how the people who have to live there stand it?"

By this time everybody leaned forward in their seats, wondering what awful smell I detected in their town. Then I said, "You know, it took me an hour to identify the peculiar essence brooding over your whole area. Then, at last, I recognized the long-forgotten odor I was smelling—*clean air!*"

They laughed with relief—but the little joke had a built-in truth. By now the whole earth has a rotten atmosphere that would seem unbearable if we hadn't been forced to adjust to it. Do you know that sin stinks? The foul works of that old serpent and his demon helpers have an odor all their own. For example, there's a dank, ugly smell to nightclubs. It's a mixture of stale, rotten beer, cigarette butts, and evil. We could bottle it under the label "Eau de Sin," but I don't think it would sell too well. Then there's the stench of Satan-induced cancer, gangrene, and vomit—the smell of hospitals.

Sin, rot, and death emit odors mindful of the "foul spirits" Jesus spoke about. Since we earthlings have never lived in an atmosphere free from human and demonic pollution, we're going to have an overwhelming and glorious reaction to Millennium's fragrance!

Did you know God has a delicate sense of smell? He speaks often of frankincense, spices, the sweet-scented trees and the flowers of Lebanon. We catch a hint of God's character exuding from His lovely flower blossoms. Sensing the person of Jesus, the Psalmist wrote, **All thy garments smell of myrrh, and aloes, and cassia** (Psalm 45:8).

I believe every one of our five senses seem to come alive at the moment of our resurrection. New fragrances will strike our whole being like an exquisite musical chord because our entire being will be in peace and perfection! When we're sick, worried, or just plain tired, nothing much feels, tastes, looks, smells, or sounds good. But when we are rested, healthy, and happy, all our senses take on new dimensions. We say, "Everything seems rosy." Imagine the "high voltage" of our new Millennium senses! Only then will we know what *real living* is all about.

When immortality surges through us, it will quicken our bodies with a bolt of resurrection life. We will pulse with new vitality and infinite new capacities to savor God's people, His angels, and His kingdom. The body is sown in weakness, but it is raised in *power*. (See 1 Corinthians 15:43.) That's Jesus' power! We will throb with pleasant new energies. We will want to skip and explore His creation.

Get ready for the life of full-spectrum gusto in the Millennium.

CHAPTER 12

ONE HOUR WITH JESUS

Wouldn't it be breathtaking to sit down with Jesus and ask Him all about the Millennium? Back when the disciples asked Him about the future, He responded with great patience and graciousness. It's always pleasing to the Lord when we show a sincere hunger for truth.

Blessed are they which do hunger and thirst after righteousness: for they shall be filled. Matthew 5:6

After Jesus had illuminated the Scriptures on the road to Emmaus, His two pupils sighed,

Did not our heart burn within us, while he talked with us? Luke 24:32

In the very opening of Revelation, we sense the Lord's honoring a desire for truth:

Blessed is he that readeth, and they that hear the
words of this prophecy, and keep those things which
are written therein: for the time is at hand. Revelation 1:3

There is a similar promise at the beginning of the longest Psalm:

Blessed are they...that seek him
with the whole heart. Psalm 119:2

Believers are encouraged to ask for wisdom and, accordingly, we should never hesitate to ask the Lord for spiritual answers. (See James 1:5.) He honors diligent inquiries from His own, and the Millennium will be no exception. It will include some very illuminating decades of teaching.

Come, and let us go up to the mountain
of the Lord, and to the house of the God of
Jacob; and he will teach us of his ways. Micah 4:2

Let's spend a hypothetical hour with Jesus right now to gain a better understanding of what life will really be like in the Millennium.

Question: "Jesus, what kind of clothes will we be wearing during the Millennium?"

Answer: "The saints will be easily distinguishable from non-glorified people by their clothing, as well as by their new bodies. Only believers will be allowed to wear the **fine linen, clean** and white: for the fine linen is the righteousness of saints (Revelation 19:8).

"The shining white of the saints will be their distinctive privilege among all that live in the renewed earth. **They shall walk with me in white: for they are worthy. He that overcometh, the same shall be clothed in white raiment** (Revelation 3:4-5).

"Again in Revelation 7:9: **Lo, a great multitude, which no man could number, of all nations, and kindreds, and people, and tongues, stood before the throne, and before the Lamb, clothed with white robes.**

"The predominance of white may sound monotonous to you, but it won't be! Those garments of white, fashioned just for you, will be stunning! These exquisite whites will signify not only your righteousness, but also your position in My kingdom."

Question: "How will we know You? What will You be wearing?"

Answer: "You will recognize Me, for it says of My garments, **thou art clothed with honor and majesty, who coverest thyself with *light* as with a garment** (Psalm 104:1-2)."

Question: "A thousand years seems so long. What will we be doing all that time?"

Answer: "It won't be a time of idleness. It is written, **his servants shall serve him** (Revelation 22:3). Just as Adam was given responsibility over the earth, so will the redeemed be privileged to serve Me. Many thrilling things will fill your new life. You will rule over earth's restoration and help govern.

There are many worlds to explore—you will never exhaust the intricacies of My universe. You'll also occupy the ages to come with the study of My principles and ways. But don't worry, you won't feel overworked. You will enjoy the boundless new energy of immortality. You'll have ample opportunities for happy meetings with redeemed friends from back in time and visits with millions from your new royal family. Then you and I will have times of fellowship, and we won't overlook games and leisure either."

Question: "Will we be able to see the angels?"

Answer: "Yes, you will see angels. Certain angels will help at the close of Armageddon. When you are changed in that 'twinkling of an eye,' your vision spectrum will be wonderfully expanded. Many spirit beings are about you even now, but in your present state they aren't yet visible. I have, in special situations, allowed saints to see angels, but glorified eyes will always be able to view them.

"In fact, you will even be sitting in court over certain angels: **Do ye not know that the saints shall judge the world? and if the world shall be judged by you, are ye unworthy to judge the smallest matters? Know ye not that we shall judge angels?** (1 Corinthians 6:2-3). You will delight in meeting My wonderful angelic creations who, although unseen in the past, often ministered in your behalf. You will meet the angel messenger I sent to Daniel: **His body also was like the beryl, and his face as the appearance of lightning, and his eyes as lamps of fire, and his arms and** his feet like in colour to polished brass, and the voice of his words like the voice of a multitude (Daniel 10:6)."

Question: "This may seem a small thing, but I've wondered if the sounds we hear will be any different in the Millennium?"

Answer: "The world is now filled with many distressing, grating noises. They are the harsh sounds of a dying age. Many people are becoming deaf because of the loud noises that are characteristic of this era's final days—the roar of motorcycles and trucks, screeching tires, blaring horns, curses, and screaming jets. Screams, weeping, arguments, and lying will never again be heard. These raucous sounds will disappear.

"The snarling, roaring, and growling animals will then have new voices of contentment, reflecting their changed natures. And when you hear the new millennial instruments and harmonies, they will transcend the greatest melodies ever to bathe the human soul. Even the Millennium's 'quiet' will pulsate with a kind of joy and tranquillity."

Question: "Will everybody be the same age in the Millennium?"

Answer: "Those who aren't glorified believers will be of various ages. **There shall yet old men and old women dwell in the streets of Jerusalem, and every man with his staff in his hand for every age. And the streets of the city shall be full of boys and girls playing** (Zechariah 8:4-5). But among my glorified family there will be perpetual youthfulness and vitality."

Question: "Will millennial citizens build houses and hold land during the new age?"

Answer: "Oh yes. **And they shall build houses, and inhabit them; and they shall plant vineyards, and eat the fruit of them. They shall not build, and another inhabit...plant, and another eat...and mine elect shall long enjoy the work of their hands...for they are the seed of the blessed of the Lord, and their offspring with them** (Isaiah 65:21-23).

"And so you see, there will be work and houses and fields, but it will be a pleasant, productive, and enchanting life. Never again will men sweat or labor fruitlessly. The new fertility of the land, the harmony with nature, and the absence of insects will make farming exciting."

Question: "Many have wondered if there will be sexual relations as we know them now during the Millennium?"

Answer: "There will be children born among the non-glorified mass of people, but for My own royal family there will be even greater ecstasies. The sexual aspect of human relationships has been the most perverted of all My designs for humanity. Sex has been so abused it has become a stench to My nostrils!

"It is not yet time for you to know the full design of the new age. But of this be assured: There will be *fullness of joy!* Every good thing experienced during this present flawed age will have a finer counterpart when you are with Me. Read again the Song of Solomon with a pure and holy heart. My patterns and principles will not be abandoned in eternity, for they are right and pleasing to Me."

Question: "Since the last enemy, death, isn't conquered until after the Millennium, does this mean that millions will die during this coming era?"

Answer: "Yes, there will be deaths among the unsaved citizens, yet death will not be found among the glorified saints, who will have new, resurrected bodies. **In a moment, in the twinkling of an eye, at the last trump...the dead shall be raised incorruptible, and we shall be changed. For this corruptible must put on incorruption, and this mortal must put on immortality. So when this corruptible shall have put on incorruption, and this mortal shall have put on immortality, then shall be brought to pass the saying that is written, Death is swallowed up in victory. O death, where is thy sting? O grave, where is thy victory?** (1 Corinthians 15:52-55)."

Question: "In the Scriptures there appear to be differences in the rewards and the rulership assignments during the Millennium. These seem related to each Christian's overall spiritual performance in this present life. Wouldn't this mean that when these heavenly prizes are given out that the apostles, martyrs, Bible heroes, and famous ministers would get the lion's share? What will be left for ordinary Christians?"

Answer: "The day in which believers' rewards are presented will bring much excitement and many surprises. Some of the so-called 'big name' Christians will receive lesser awards than expected. **For other foundation can no man lay than that is laid, which is Jesus Christ. Now if any man build** upon this foundation gold, silver, precious stones, wood, hay, stubble; every man s work shall be made manifest: for the day shall declare it, because it shall be revealed by fire; and the fire shall try every man s work of what sort it is. If any man s work abide which he hath built thereupon, he shall receive a reward (1 Corinthians 3:11-14).

"The *heart motive* behind everything done in My name will be a strong factor in determining spiritual rewards. **That which is highly esteemed among men is abomination in the sight of God** (Luke 16:15). Work to please God, not to impress others. **Not with eyeservice, as menpleasers; but as the servants of Christ, doing the will of God from the heart** (Ephesians 6:6).

"Also, there will be amazement when I present special rewards to presently unknown men, women, and children. Many who are unheralded have quietly demonstrated great spiritual dedication and valor! Their spiritual heroism is frequently unrecognized in this life. **Many that are first shall be last; and the last shall be first** (Matthew 19:30).

"Some 'little' people who never led anyone into salvation will still be found near the front in the reward line. There will be those who, for many years, labored in prayer while stricken with pain and even bedridden. Others will be singled out for heavenly acclaim who have allowed the Holy Spirit to develop in them a fragrant spiritual character during an earthly life filled with adversities.

"Heroes will be revealed who were steadfast in the midst of prison and torture. Godly women who remained aglow with the Spirit though for many years linked to a wicked, abusing mate will be rewarded. And many faithful shepherds of small flocks who never knew acclaim will be given assignments of great responsibility because they proved faithful in the small things. Crowning Day will ring throughout eternity! Thomas Gray understood this in his poem:

> *Full many a gem of purest ray serene*
> *The dark, unfathomed caves of ocean bear:*
> *Full many a flower is born to blush unseen,*
> *And waste its sweetness on the desert air.*"

Question: "This, again, may seem like a tiny thing, but I love to fish. Will there be any fishing in the kingdom age?"

Answer: "Millennium fishing will be the very best! **And it will come about that every living creature which swarms in every place where the river goes, will live. And there will be very many fish, for these waters go there, and the others become fresh, so everything will live where the river goes. And it will come about that fishermen will stand beside it; from Engedi to Eneglaim there will be a place for the spreading of nets. Their fish will be according to their kinds** (Ezekiel 47:9-10 NASB)."

Question: "It seems hazardous for the glorified believers to live here on earth during the Millennium among those who haven't yet been changed. Won't the behavior of some tempt the glorified to sin?"

Answer: "No, that won't be any problem whatsoever. The glorified believer will have put off corruption and put on incorruption. By then, the glorified have been transformed and sealed against even any impure thoughts. This new and permanent incorruption will be essential so that My redeemed may be sent safely anywhere. They will be required to rule and reign in many kinds of situations."

"Thank You, Lord."

CHAPTER 13

SIX CRISES OF GOD

We would not do justice to this millennial study without touching upon one vital issue. How should God have dealt with His chronic problem of people and sin? His centuries-long forbearance with humanity reveals His matchless character. By now it's clear that He will complete His ages-old plan for earth in spite of man! If shortsighted humanity had been responsible for harmony in the universe and had all power, they would have long ago pressed the earth's "destruct" button.

The English word "holy" has an interesting root origin. It's derived from the Old English *halig*, which meant "whole." Holiness is to divine creation what breath is to life. A. W. Tozer, in his book, *The Knowledge of the Holy*, said,

> God's first concern for His universe is its moral health, that is, its holiness. Whatever is contrary brings His displeasure. To preserve creation, God must deal with anything that would destroy it. When

He arises to put down iniquity and save the world
from moral collapse, He is said to be angry. Every
act of judgment in the history of the world has
instead been a holy move for its own preservation.
The holiness of God, the judgments of God, and the
health of the creation are inseparable. God's wrath is
His utter intolerance of whatever degrades and
destroys men. He hates iniquity as a mother hates
the polio that would take the life of her child.

Earth is polluted from a 6,000-year outfall of man's unholi-
ness. God's patience in sparing earth is amazing, but in that
patience is buried a colossal plan. A divine pattern is at work to
restore both humanity and their planet to the idyllic beginning.

The shadow of God's ways has been evident from the start.
Heaven itself opened with a perfect society. There was harmony
and great purpose. The Father's galactic building programs alone
would have kept things exciting—a place of purposeful harmony.

But eventually God desired to expand this family, that His
joy might be still greater. Yet how? God's nature could never
find satisfaction from mere robot-like love and obedience.
Desiring a relationship of choice, God energized one of His
most colossal thoughts: *free will*. But when He chose to incorporate this free-will principle into His creation, the potential
for rebellion was also born. Each of the six great crises of God
emanate from this divine latitude.

But aren't you glad our great Lord stayed with His bold
free-will concept? How much sweeter to God is our freely
given love than "automatic reflex" love. How exciting to be

creatures entrusted with our own will rather than captive, preprogrammed robots. The price He has paid in creature disobedience to obtain this sweeter love, however, has been ongoing and enormous! If a lesser being had been sitting at the controls of the universe, he would have washed his hands long ago, saying, "Making humans was a good try, but...."

But not our God! He looked right through all the crises and saw eventual victory. It is because of His long-range vision that humanity has been permitted to survive in spite of its sin. Aren't you glad He never quit on His creation?

Satan has been the evil quarterback calling the plays behind each one of these crises. As we briefly review these six major rebellions, marvel at God's display of love and persistence.

CRISIS 1

Its battle cry: **I will be like the most High** (Isaiah 14:14).

Location: Heaven

Participants: Angels

Top-ranking angel Lucifer personally led the very first revolt. One-third of the heavenly family followed this lawless one in defection from the Holy One:

> *Thine heart was lifted up because of thy beauty,*
> *thou has corrupted thy wisdom by reason of thy*
> *brightness: I will cast thee to the ground, I will lay thee*
> *before kings, that they may behold thee.* Ezekiel 28:17

Yes, there was lawlessness in spite of a perfect environment. This huge band of angel outlaws was cast from God's presence in heaven and earth became their "turf." The heavenly Father brushed His hands and moved right on with His master plan....

CRISIS 2

Its battle cry: **Ye shall be as gods** (Genesis 3:5).

Location: The Garden of Eden

Participants: Adam and Eve

Again, idyllic conditions. Adam and Eve had total freedom from sickness, poverty, sweat, and strain. God vested earthly authority in Adam and walked with him in the cool of the day. The Lord laid down simple rules of life for Adam, but Satan connived to snare him into violating them. Satan set a trap and Adam fell! After this satanic victory, sin infected Adam and Eden. That violation cost Adam his title deed to earth. Satan had snatched it away, and God's curse fell upon the planet. Now humanity faced massive new obstacles. The Father had to break person-to-person contact with sin-contaminated man.

Even so, God chose to move on with His blueprint....

CRISIS 3

Its battle cry: **My spirit shall not always strive with man** (Genesis 6:3).

Location: Beyond Eden

Participants: Antediluvian Civilization (before the great flood)

God allowed many benefits to continue from the Eden era. However, it wasn't long until that sin virus had spread throughout the earth and **every imagination of the thoughts of [men s] heart[s] was only evil continually** (Genesis 6:5). The world became filled with despicable lewdness and violence. God saw such utter moral collapse that a complete new start for humanity was the only hope.

Through Noah's preaching God urged repentance and warned of coming doom. Noah built an ark of rescue to preserve a seed of humanity. All humanity except for Noah's family laughed at God and "revved up" their debauchery:

> *The earth also was corrupt before God, and
> the earth was filled with violence.* Genesis 6:11

God mercifully sent the waters, and the rebellious, diseased, and violent were lost in the deluge Noah had prophesied. Humanity came within a tiny handful of utter extinction because of its defiance.

And still, God wasn't dissuaded from the great plan....

CRISIS 4

Its battle cry: "We will not have this Man to rule over us!" (See John 1:11.)

Location: Middle East

Participants: All humanity

It is incredible that God continued to put up with man. His ways surely are above our ways—God is no quitter! Thousands of years went by after the flood. God's heart was touched as He watched humanity struggling in failure. People were living on a spiritual battlefield, caught in the crossfire between Satan and God. God saw some whose hearts were inclined toward righteousness, but they were in bondage to the prince of this world.

Then God launched "Operation Rescue"! He brought forth His most valuable possession—His own Son—to serve as a ransom. His life was the only payment sufficient to repurchase sinful people. The Son personally went to the cross to discharge our own debt for sin. Jesus came to destroy the works of the devil and was imminently successful. This God-sized plan shattered Satan's death-grip on humanity!

You would think this colossal sacrifice would forever break the string of crises between God and man, but it still didn't end there:

> *He came unto his own, and his*
> *own received him not. John 1:11*

They shouted, "We will not have this Man to rule over us." They crucified Him, but He rose in triumph, making a display of Satan's defeat.

The fourth terrible crisis had come and the Good Seed had been sown. The Lord pressed on....

CRISIS 5

Its battle cry: "They blasphemed God and repented not of their deeds." (See Revelation 9:20-21.)

Location: Worldwide

Participants: Satan and the Sinners

Even though God's Calvary-stroke didn't bring instant heaven, Jesus' work on planet earth bore much lasting fruit. The seeds of victory had been sown—God's Word, the Bible, was scattered through humanity. On Pentecost the Holy Spirit filled believers to spread the Good News to the ends of the earth. Yet with all God had done for humanity, trouble looms again as people have chosen Satan's evil over God's salvation until the world is ripe for a global Sodom and Gomorrah!

God's justice must always stand against wickedness. The vague hope that God is too kind ever to punish the unrighteous has become a deadly tranquilizer. It soothes the sinner's fears and lets him practice all pleasant iniquities while death draws nearer every day. God cannot and will not tolerate wickedness, for it would destroy His creation if allowed to spread unchecked.

And this rebellion does not end until **the great and the terrible day of the Lord** (Joel 2:31). History's most horrendous war—Armageddon—is stilled only by the appearance of Jesus Christ. The sinister leader of malevolent forces is literally chained and God's fifth great crisis will end.

The near-idyllic Millennium era then opens, and Jesus sets up shop on earth. Mankind is given 1,000 Satan-free years to decide its eternal allegiance. The final exams then take place....

CRISIS 6

Its battle cry: "We will follow Satan and not the King!" (See Revelation 20:7-9.)

Location: Jerusalem

Participants: Satan and the Last Dregs of Sinful Humanity

Note that there are *six* major crises. Six is the number of incompleteness and it is also the number of humanity. Mankind will always be frustrated and incomplete until they add one more element to their lives—Jesus. *Seven* is the number of perfection and also the number of divinity. Whenever humanity has tried to go it alone, with humanity as god, they have failed. Whenever they have tried to be masters of their own fate and captain of their own souls, they have crashed. Human beings become warlike, sickened, and miserable when God is crowded out.

The sixth and final rebellion will take place around Jerusalem. At the very end of the Millennium, Satan is again loosed to roam among humanity. As incredible as it seems, Satan will actually be able to recruit an army for a final war against the saints at Jerusalem. These rebellious Millenniumites will be recruited from among the children born to the non-glorified populace. Satan and his wicked army will storm Jerusalem itself.

Finally, though, God will have had enough. He will reach for that "destruct" button! Fire will rain from heaven and every last rebel will be forever eliminated. Satan will be thrown into the lake of fire and the testing times will be forever behind us. Those remaining will have passed their final exams and graduated into eternity.

At that point, the great circle of God will be completed. His royal household will have grown to include every person, through all the ages, whose hearts inclined toward Him. We'll be a great family, tested and proven under fire. Through faith each will have personally chosen to join the family of God. A joyous Father will extend full royal privileges to His family forever!

Thou art worthy, O Lord, to receive glory and honour and power: for thou hast created all things, and for thy pleasure they are and were created. Revelation 4:11

CHAPTER 14

SCIENTIFIC SAGA

During the Millennium, science and technology will reach their stratospheric zeniths! In recent years, many Christians have imagined that scientific progress was totally at odds with the spiritual. Perhaps this misconception arose because many in the academic world are avid attackers of God's Word. Most college campuses have become hotbeds of anti-God teaching. When science and technology began to peak, a trend to exalt the creature more than the Creator also emerged. However, all that science discovers, God lays claim to as His own thought and design:

> *Thus saith the Lord, thy redeemer, and he that formed thee from the womb, I am the Lord that maketh all things; that stretcheth forth the heavens alone; that spreadeth abroad the earth by myself.* Isaiah 44:24

The Bible foresaw our present-day scientific advances:

Even to the time of the end...knowledge
shall be increased. Daniel 12:4

But Satan tirelessly works to pervert every good thing. He fans the flame of sinful human pride to cry, "I am the master of my fate and the captain of my soul!" thus encouraging humanity to become cocky about their accomplishments. Beginning during the early triumphs of the space age, a near worship of science arose. As knowledge has increased exponentially, so has man's pride. The prince of this world will use anything to divert our worship away from God to our own accomplishments.

Man has never, in a full sense of the word, created anything. That's a pretty strong statement, but a true one. Science and technology merely apply God's existing laws of nature and work with existing materials supplied by God. "But," people point out, "we've made giant leaps in technology and science since the turn of this century. We've seen a cascade of startling developments: the telephone, radio, automobile, airplane, atomic energy, laser, computer, television, and space flight. Why shouldn't we be proud?"

Have these great achievements forever angered God and violated our relationship with Him? Of course not! People are working with the elements and energies He has already placed here. It was the Lord who commanded us to "subdue the earth" and who said, "Do whatsoever you do with all your might as unto Me." (See Colossians 3:23.)

It was God who designed and created the incredible human brain, and who put us here to rule the planet. Imagine what a colossal civilization we would be enjoying if Adam hadn't allowed mind-polluting sin to degenerate the human species. Sin has obstructed the full flow of human progress.

But do you realize how many great scientific breakthroughs have occurred through God's inspiration? Only from the perspective of eternity will we discover the extent of divine inspiration behind many modern achievements. There are countless testimonies of supernaturally inspired inventions among Christians working in the fields of engineering and science. A host of great men and women openly credit God for scientific insights following prayer.

R. G. LeTourneau built heavy earth-moving equipment for vast projects like the Hoover Dam. He always spoke of his "Senior Partner" who inspired and enlightened him throughout his career. Once, while LeTourneau was flying home in his private plane, he fell asleep. About thirty minutes into his nap, LeTourneau took a small notebook from his pocket and jotted a note, then returned to sleep. As they were landing, a business associate asked him if he remembered writing a note during the flight.

"Oh, did I?" said LeTourneau. He pulled out the notebook and laughed. "Here it is! This is the solution to a problem I've had with a machine! I've been looking for this answer for weeks, and now my Senior Partner has supplied it!"

This shouldn't come as a surprise. In James 1:5 we read,

If any of you lack wisdom, let him ask of God,
that giveth to all men liberally…and it shall be given him.

Most of us have, at one time or another, felt divine inspiration. If satanic inspiration can move the medium and the murderer, then godly inspiration can direct a Christian engineer.

NASA scientist Dr. Rodney Johnson is another modern example. He has told of his years at General Electric when the Lunar Excursion Module (LEM) was under development. The LEM was essential to the Apollo program because it would transport the astronauts down to the surface of the moon. Even more critical, the LEM flies the men back up for a precision rendezvous with the command ship. A failure would leave the astronauts stranded on the moon.

The intricate LEM would have to be extremely light and compact, able to be carried on the long journey to the moon. It would have to incorporate great power, reliability, and maneuverability to fulfill its delicate role. The exotic vehicle had to incorporate full life-support systems for its two-man crew and also serve as a space truck—carrying the tools, test equipment, and even a lunar rover. The space link would then have to provide constant communication to the mother ship and incorporate fail-safe re-docking features.

These design requirements seemed impossible! When this took place in the 1970s, we all became so fascinated with the powerful booster rockets and the Apollo command ship that we overlooked the stupendous engineering challenges involved in building a reliable Lunar Excursion Module.

Johnson told of the agonizing mental strain that went into the LEM's development. Its designers faced a maze of engineering obstacles. They were pushing far beyond the present state of the art. At virtually every point they needed components, electronics, and materials that didn't yet exist. So Johnson and several other Christian engineers prayed together each morning prior to work. Before picking up a slide rule or punching a computer key, they gathered and prayed for wisdom. Slowly, these technical barriers started to fall in response to their barrages of prayer. Johnson attributed the LEM's brilliant success to their partnership with God in its conception.

Today we have dramatically moved beyond that original Apollo moonwalk. Through the years, many other Christian scientists have made great strides in exploration of the galaxies beyond the moon and give God credit for their successes.

HALL OF FAME

Johannes Kepler was a brilliant German theoretician who worked closely with the foremost astronomers of his day. He unlocked the secret of the planets' paths, discovering how they move in ellipses. The science of astronomy is grounded on Kepler's laws of planetary motion.

Kepler was a fervent, praying Christian as well as an authentic genius. Some years ago his personal-work diaries were found, and a learned team of scholars hastily assembled to translate his material for inclusion in modern science textbooks. The translators were baffled as they struggled with the great physicist's brilliant material. They couldn't tell whether his work was religious or scientific. Kepler would write in his work log a paragraph of intricate equations, then alternate with a paragraph of praises to the Lord! No wonder God shared great cosmic mysteries with Kepler.

Michael Faraday was a physicist without peer. The electrical measurement called the *farad* is named after this eminent scientist. For twenty years he interpreted his brilliant scientific achievements with the preaching of the Gospel—every single Sunday!

Sir Isaac Newton formulated the law of gravity—that masses attract each other with a force directly proportional to weight and inversely proportional to the square of the distance apart. It is to Sir Isaac we owe the familiar, "For every action there is an equal and opposite reaction." Newton also built the first reflecting telescope and discovered that a prism separates light into its component colors. But, first and foremost, Isaac Newton was a fervent disciple of Jesus Christ. He spent the last decade of his life writing an extensive exposition on biblical prophecy and the end times.

THE FEARSOME GENIE

What is mankind's principle gain through the recent explosion of knowledge? *Trouble,* that's what! But why trouble? Because humanity is sinful, selfish, and at enmity with their Creator. In our present vulnerable state, many great scientific achievements have been turned around and used to harm mankind.

Our scientific growth has outpaced our moral character. Today, at the very pinnacle of scientific attainment, our planet is wracked with violence, disease, hunger, and hate. Chemical advances have given us not only new medicines and wonder materials, but also methamphetamine and napalm bombs! The invention of motion pictures was an immediate delight to man. Before long, however, films began to spread unspeakable moral pollution by glorifying violence, perversion, and filth.

Yes, we have abused the fruits of science. It was a treacherous thing to let the scientific genie out of the bottle while man was still so in league with evil. Ever since the first murder by Cain, sinful people have feverishly worked to invent better and better slaughtering tools. One breakthrough after another vested temporary advantage to its inventors. It has been so from the crossbow to suitcase nuclear weapons! Too much of our "subduing of the earth" is now centered in the scientific disciplines of warfare. The "genie" has already created enough destructive power to enable us to blast our own planet off its axis!

It's true that scientific discoveries in themselves don't offend God, but their perverse usage does. These incredible disciplines, however, will find outlet for the blessing of humanity when, at Millennium's dawn,

They shall beat their swords into plowshares,
and their spears into pruninghooks...neither
shall they learn war any more. Isaiah 2:4

Come quickly, Lord Jesus!

Chapter 15

Supermind

Thought and speech are God's gift to man, intimately associated with Him and impossible without Him.
—A. W. Tozer

The mind is an astounding creation. It's a maze of intricate circuitry linking some 20 billion neurons and 160 billion glial cells. The brain still has not been duplicated, even with dozens of the most advanced high-speed computers. Imagine the human brain: 180 billion parts smoothly linked and silently powered by electrochemistry. The entire wondrous machine is neatly housed in a small, bone-protected sphere—the ultimate in micro-miniaturization! If there were nothing else by which to glimpse the incredible brilliance of God, the human brain should suffice.

Neurosurgeons and behavioral science researchers say the incredible human brain is now functioning at less than 7 percent of its design capacity. I believe this loss of mental efficiency stems directly from the fall of man through sin. But since we have seen such brilliant accomplishments while using only a fraction of our brains, imagine what we can do when our unshackled Millennium minds are turned loose in science and technology.

Arthur Longley has brilliantly comprehended the electrifying surge of new mental energy believers will soon experience. He says,

> We ought to make it perfectly clear that immortality is not a rest-cure for nervous wrecks in a parkland rehabilitation center, 50 billion miles away, but instead it is God's practical scheme to reshape civilization for the common good of mankind. Suddenly, at the Rapture, the Christian will inherit a life force that will stimulate the brain to high levels of intelligence, capable of grappling with the problems that now baffle the world's greatest minds.

It is no small thing that the massive scientific efforts now concentrating on weapons research and on curing disease can then be directed toward the blessing of humanity. It is not difficult to forecast presently unimaginable benefits accruing to millennial civilization as a result of new teams of ultra-brilliant minds focusing on constructive developments.

Millennial brainpower will get further boost as a result of the mind's being coupled with vibrantly healthy bodies. The human being is a complex system with vast numbers of inter-related subsystems. For example, a weak, diseased body hampers the efficiency of the mind. Fear, tensions, and sickness war against the perfect operation of the mind. Sin affects our mental engine like sand affects gears. When sin is banished, the mind will blossom.

There will be phenomenal consequences from this sudden unshackling of human creativity. We see it in Jesus' life, and Isaiah explains it comes from God's Spirit:

> *The spirit of wisdom and understanding...*
> *the spirit of knowledge...shall make him*
> *quick of understanding.* Isaiah 11:2-3

This "touch" in our minds will bring giant leaps in the fields of communication, transportation, energy, and agriculture. Shall we consider a few of these exciting possibilities?

The world is troubled by limitations in the supply and distribution of petroleum. Many are worrying about what we'll do to fuel our cars, ships, airplanes, and electric generating stations. Statisticians gloomily foresee lights dimming and wheels and engines sputtering to a stop. But we have a Creator whose schedules and timetables are always perfect! I believe that before all of earth's gears lock up for want of lubrication, this age will close. Without doubt, the oil supplies that God placed on the planet will prove adequate to squeak through this era.

Then I expect to see millennial technical breakthroughs provide the new world with inexhaustible, pollution-free energy alternatives. Scientists know that a glass of water has more potential energy locked in its molecular structures than a million barrels of oil or 100,000 tons of coal. They just can't unlock it yet. We will see that secret unlocked to provide unlimited, pollution-free power in the age to come.

The technology of the new age, with perhaps advanced fusion engines or hydrogen-oxygen fuel cell power, will provide efficient, clean, silent propulsion. The ecologists will love the Millennium. The Millennium will at last see an ecological utopia.

MILLENNIAL MAGIC CARPETS

Congestion, accidents, and pollution are consequences of our overcrowded streets and groaning transportation systems. Twentieth-century man still travels almost exclusively in one hilly, congested plane—the earth's surface. This will be corrected. Even with the thousands of aircraft now flying, our skies are still largely unused. There are hundreds of additional transportation corridors in the air above us.

We will be traveling these airways in public supersonic airbuses or our own nifty aircars. This will enable us to swiftly and effortlessly go anywhere. We will see new engines, advanced metallurgy, even tinier computers, more advanced navigation satellites, laser landing systems and revolutionized aerodynamics. Fast and easy-to-fly vehicles will be as easy to build as our mass-produced automobiles.

It isn't difficult to visualize a six-passenger supersonic aircar that would be driven as easily as we now pilot our own cars. With automated flight controls and landing systems, it will be possible to program Beijing for lunch and be on our way.

Millennial aircars will hover and land effortlessly, parking in our own garage.

Computers will direct beautiful air freighters, perhaps a mile, long through their own assigned air corridors. They will move fresh food, materials, and even houses—playing their part in ideal logistics and distribution for all of the millennial civilization.

Today's scenery is marred by millions of ugly telephone poles and power transmission lines. Millennial life will not require such crude interconnecting systems. Every building will have its own compact power unit built in, which will supply all its needs. Likewise, there will be no phones or other communications systems that are not completely wireless. Today with our cell phones, Iridium satellite phones, and the Internet, instant global communications are possible, but full of glitches.

Not so in the Millennium! We "Millenniumites" will carry our own pocket televisions so we won't miss the stream of news from the world capital, Jerusalem! With these pocket portables, we can watch the breathtaking millennial transformations taking place around the world. "Behold, all things become new"—and right before our eyes! And the content of that television will be revolutionized. Good news will be a hallmark of the age. The present "Bad News Broadcasting Network" will be out of business. Perhaps newscasts from other parts of the universe will be one of the exciting Kingdom Age features.

New interest in the wholesome will replace the present macabre fascination with evil and violent news. No longer will men have such an appetite for the works of darkness. Won't it be nifty to get broadcasts devoid of sex, war, famine, murder, rape, robbery, riots, hate, and corrupt politicians? The telecasts we will hear will crackle with exciting good news!

MIRACLE MEMORY

Flawless memories will be characteristic of the millennial mind. Won't that be a neat bonus? How often we have yearned to quickly remember the names of acquaintances! During the Millennium, we'll not only remember everything, we'll even instantly recognize the saints from past generations. Paul understood this. He looked forward to a future where his knowledge burst its present boundaries:

> *But then shall I know even as*
> *also I am known.* 1 Corinthians 13:12

Won't it be something to talk to new old friends like Noah, Peter, Jonathan, and David? We will know them just like Peter instantly knew Moses and Elijah on the Mount of Transfiguration. (See Luke 9.) And how great it will be to chat with more new friends like Martin Luther and those unnamed martyrs of the Roman coliseum.

We will remember everything we need to remember—dates, anniversaries, appointments. No more time wasted hunting lost items. Never again will we forget important facts or lessons. We will experience no more "blanks" in our mind.

BABEL REVERSED

Another exciting change will bring great joy and new efficiency to mankind during the Millennium—a new language. According to Wycliffe Bible Translators, there are more than 6,700 different known languages in the world today. What a terrible toll in frustration and misunderstanding these thousands of tongues have caused us! God sent this confusion of tongues upon humanity as judgment for their pride and arrogance in building the Tower of Babel. (See Genesis 11.) But He has also promised,

> *For then will I turn to the people a pure language,*
> *that they may all call upon the name of the Lord,*
> *to serve him with one consent.* *Zephaniah 3:9*

Can you hear everybody praising Jesus in the same language?

THE TIME MUSEUM

From the moment we are born we have to wage a running fight with sickness and death. Particularly for those now battling pain, the coming glory holds special promise. Instant renewal of aching and aging bodies is imminent, and it can't come too soon. A weariness resides among the peoples of earth, **but they that wait upon the Lord shall renew their strength...They shall run, and not be weary...walk, and not faint** (Isaiah 40:31). And for those fighting the ancient enemy, sickness, the good news is that Jesus Christ shall change our lowly body so that it may be fashioned like His glorious body. (See Philippians 3:20-21.) That's the *ultimate* in healing! Yes, sickness and pain will have been smashed at the Rapture for every millennial saint:

> *The eyes of the blind shall be opened, and*
> *the ears of the deaf shall be unstopped.*
> *Then shall the lame man leap as an hart,*
> *and the tongue of the dumb sing.* Isaiah 35:5-6

Vibrant physical and emotional health will be the kingdom age norm! And the Millennium's perfect moral and spiritual environment will insure against any relapse. Immortality is forever!

We should ever bear in mind the two-tiered nature of millennial society. Many benefits that each glorified saint will enjoy may not be available to the non-glorified populace. For example, there will probably be death, aging, and some sickness among those who haven't exchanged corruption for incorruption.

Maybe there will be a Time Museum with displays of all those obsolete things like hearing aids, toupees, dental drills, eyeglasses, surgical tools, wheelchairs, and crutches. All these could remind us of the glory of our new estate. Every stress, heartache, and pain now encountered by the born-again Christian will have fled on Millennium morning. A clear vision of the Millennium sets our present in perspective:

> *I reckon that the sufferings of this present time*
> *are not worthy to be compared with the glory*
> *which shall be revealed in us.* Romans 8:18

CHAPTER 16

MISSION CONTROL

The Bible makes it clear that Jesus chose to work during His 33 remarkable years on earth as the Son of *Man*. He dramatically proved what a sin-free person could accomplish while acting in harmony with God. Jesus boldly divested Himself of divine advantages and functioned in the same sin-charged environment we know.

But if Jesus worked as the Son of Man, how did He perform all those miracles—rebuking storms, raising the dead, walking on water, multiplying bread—and how did the man Jesus know about the past life of the woman at the well? He has freely told His secret, and His followers have spread the Word around the world, but men are still unwilling to pay the price to do as He did. Yet the opportunity is still open to us.

What were His victory secrets? Although Jesus experienced the same temptations we do, He never allowed the world's sin-drenched environment to overcome Him. This purity kept the "hotline" to His Father wide open. Did you ever realize that purity actually generates power? Yes, power arises from purity and obedience. Asceticism or good works have no dynamic, only a godly, genuine righteousness. Because of Jesus' perfect obedience and His perfect holiness, He had an unbroken power line to all the resources of the Father.

Jesus often said, in effect, "All that I do, the Father showed Me." By disciplining every earthly impulse and acting in harmony with the Father, Jesus retained the constant backing of heaven. No wonder He could do such mighty works, even though He limited Himself as the Son of Man.

Several years ago Russ Busby, the photographer for World-Wide Pictures, was shooting stills at Pat Boone's home in Beverly Hills. After the picture session was over, Russ, Pat, and I drifted into a very stimulating discussion about this relationship between Jesus and His Father. We talked about how, during the Apollo project, the world saw a beautiful working harmony between Mission Control and the astronauts. Mission Control at the Johnson Space Flight Center in Houston was constantly available for guidance during their efforts out in space, and the communication link between the astronauts and the center was absolutely essential to every mission success.

The resources at Mission Control constantly backed up the astronauts. The training, the backing, the obedience of the astronauts, and their instant hotline to the space center made possible the string of breathtaking space successes! And during the Apollo 13 mission, that hotline was a lifeline, as the experts at Mission Control devised a way to save the astronauts in their explosion-damaged spacecraft.

So it was with Jesus. During His work down here on the planet earth, Jesus too was continuously backed by heavenly "Mission Control" with all His wisdom, resources, and unlimited power. By maintaining purity in His life and, thereby, a constant access to the power of heaven, Jesus moved victoriously, even in the midst of this world's sin environment. No wonder He performed such incredible feats!

This victory formula will work for us too. We also qualify for that instant backing of the Father **that whatsoever ye shall ask of the Father in my name, he may give it you** (John 15:16). Through prayer, we can call on the same resources Jesus tapped into. When operating in harmony with God's Word, Christians can see a fulfillment of Jesus' startling promise, "greater things shall ye do." (See John 14:12.)

LATENT POWER OF THE MIND

Because we who walk in the Spirit have the mind of Christ, Jesus' mind also merits our attention. (See 1 Corinthians 2:16.) That is an amazing truth that easily eludes us now, but will come into sharp focus in the Millennium. Looking back from the perspective of eternity, we may be amazed to learn how much Jesus accomplished through having His mind smoothly harnessed with the Holy Spirit. Jesus' keen insights into people and situations were possible through the combination of His mind functioning at its full potential and blended with the Spirit.

Our computer-like brains are now partially "shorted out" by
sin. The effects are similar to the way man-made computers
are disabled by a cup of coffee spilled into the keyboard. Everyone
has experienced the effects on their own thinking powers when
sin enters: confusion, poor judgment, irrational thought, and
more. Worry and fear markedly affect our minds as a result of
sin. Guilt also affects the brain when sin remains unconfessed.
Over 50,000 violent deaths occur each year as a result of the
impaired mental abilities of drunk drivers. Drugs and alcohol
wreak havoc in the brain's delicate circuitry.

Since all corruption will have been put off from the glorified
saints, we can see how the transformation in the millennial
mind will enable fantastic mental accomplishments. Our new
harmony with God will likewise bring us an indescribable sense
of well-being, far exceeding the most delightful state of mind
we have ever known. Vibrant harmony among spirit, mind,
and body will explode into colossal accomplishments and
indescribable joy. Oh, the ecstasy of unbroken communication
with our Lord!

CHAPTER 17

A FOUNTAIN OF YOUTH

I suppose each of us has wondered what we, personally, will look like in the Millennium. Every year we spend in this sin-impregnated world brutalizes us. Every earth day grinds at our being like a sandstorm tearing at a flower. At one time or another, we've all peered into a mirror to examine time's relentless work...tick, tick, tick...here a deepening wrinkle, there another little strain line. Remember the mini-crisis of spotting a first gray hair? Then, ever so subtly, our eyes slip their focus. Later comes the unwelcome weariness too early in the evening...tick, tick, tick.

The wages of time yield irreversible death in the physical realm. Death starts its work the day we are born. People spend billions of dollars each year trying to fight off that old tyrant, Time. But, alas, we can only powder, patch, and dye for a season. Soon the hair dye and the cosmetics fail before Time's terrible oppression.

Men and women have paid heavily in their search for elusive fountains of youth, using elixirs, super-drugs, diets, and plastic surgery to fight back that relentless ticking clock. Well-funded geneticists work non-stop to locate the genes that control aging, so they can turn them off. But Time has never yet been denied its pay! Let's face it; wouldn't we all like to find the fountain of youth? This deep yearning is actually our spirit's God-given quest for eternal life.

This inborn desire to defy aging has inspired a lot of fancy fiction. There was once a television series called "The Six Million Dollar Man" about a man whom scientists marvelously rebuilt after a "fatal" accident. Suddenly, he could outrun horses, leap over buildings, and many other things well beyond the capabilities of mankind in the natural. Behind all the smoke of fantasy, could there be some real fire of immortality—a true fountain of youth somewhere? Here, again, truth will soon outrun fiction. When the believers' clock strikes *Rapture,* look out! A real fountain of youth will appear, at last! Paul wrote, **We ourselves groan within ourselves, waiting for the adoption, to wit, the redemption of our body** (Romans 8:23). Our fountain of youth will prove to be a translation from mortality to immortality, through Jesus. Live reality will soon transcend cold theology!

Have you been looking in that mirror and felt depressed by what you see? Then change to Jesus' mirror:

But we all, with open face beholding as in a glass the glory
of the Lord, are changed into the same image from glory
to glory, even as by the Spirit of the Lord. 2 Corinthians 3:18

Don't let the enemy ever again lay a spirit of despondency
on you because of those little aging marks. Look in God's
mirror and rejoice! Say, "Pride of Life, out with you! Any
hour now I'll be plunged into Jesus' fountain of youth! And
I'm not coming out as just some retread, but much better
than ever!" Look to Jesus, **Who shall change our vile body,**
that it may be fashioned like unto his glorious body
(Philippians 3:21). No more wrinkle cream, no more glasses,
no more girdles, no more zit creams, no more crutches, no
more diets, and no more pills! Never again will we know
insomnia, fear, pain or disappointment. Let's hear it for Jesus!

But what exactly will you look like? Will you be completely
different? Scriptures tell us,

There is a natural body, and there is a spiritual body....
And as we have borne the image of the earthy, we shall
also bear the image of the heavenly. 1 Corinthians 15:44,49

Yes, you will be different, and yet, somehow more *you* than
ever! Brace yourself—you're going to like the real you!

Will your friends recognize you? I think so. On the Mount
of Transfiguration, Peter instantly recognized the glorified
Jesus, though there was a great supernatural glow—a heavenly
quality—that emanated from His being. And when he saw

Elijah and Moses talking with Jesus, Peter immediately knew both of them. Later on, when two of Jesus' disciples walked along the road to Emmaus with the resurrected Christ, He looked to them like a man. When Mary saw Jesus outside the tomb, He didn't look like a specter but a real person, and He was. After His resurrection, Jesus led many souls back from their graves and right into the streets of Jerusalem for a short while:

> *And came out of the graves after his resurrection, and went into the holy city, and appeared unto many.* Matthew 27:53

What a nostalgic detour to experience on their way to heaven!

In another incident after His resurrection, Jesus suddenly appeared among the disciples. He invited Thomas to touch and to handle Him, saying,

> *Behold my hands and my feet, that it is I myself: handle me, and see; for a spirit hath not flesh and bones, as ye see me have.* Luke 24:39

Immediately, Thomas answered, **My Lord and my God** (John 20:28). The resurrected Jesus also participated in a fish fry on the shore of Lake Galilee, eating along with His disciples.

But the new Jesus also had some marked differences after the resurrection, didn't He? He could still function in earth's natural environment but He could also, at will, transcend it. He was no longer constrained by either gravity or matter. Jesus could appear in a room without coming through the door. Just as a television signal can freely move right through the whirling atoms of apparently solid materials, so will we after our own transformation. The disciples watched Jesus ignore the pull of gravity when He soared upward like a beautiful, silent missile from the Mount of Olives.

Earlier Jesus had demonstrated His ability to move into the regions of the dead itself. No force, no matter, no being could restrain His actions. God gave Jesus all power in heaven and in earth, and it is His will that we share this, as joint heirs, with Him. God promises believers,

> *But we know that, when he shall appear,*
> *we shall be like him.* 1 John 3:2

Are you beginning to grasp the wonder of it?

> *Behold, I shew you a mystery...we shall all be changed,*
> *In a moment, in the twinkling of an eye....*
> *for the trumpet shall sound...and we*
> *shall be changed.* 1 Corinthians 15:51-52

David caught this magnificence when he wrote, **I shall be satisfied, when I awake, with thy likeness** (Psalm 17:15).

STRATIFIED SOCIETY

The millions of non-glorified citizens of the Millennium won't be either a physical or a mental match for the saints. If they competed in such competition as sports, or even chess, they would be no match. There would have to be separate leagues. The saints would embarrass the fabled "Six Million Dollar Man" in any task—physical or mental.

But those ordinary millennial citizens will still experience great bonuses from the new era. There will be longer life.

> *There shall be no more thence an infant of days,*
> *nor an old man that hath not filled his days: for*
> *the child shall die an hundred years old.* Isaiah 65:20

Back in the Old Testament times of the patriarchs, a long life was normal. Abraham fathered Isaac when he was past 100. Moses' vital life forces were still bright when he was 120. In still earlier times, before Satan had so fully polluted humanity with sin, people lived still longer. Children were born to 700-year-old parents.

During the Millennium, I believe the non-glorified will experience three pluses over that Methuselah era of longevity: first, Jesus will be present on earth; second, Satan will be totally out of business; and third, no wicked people will be allowed to corrupt society. However, in the Millennium mortals who don't accept the saving grace of Jesus will die because until earth's re-creation, death will remain.

Since God has always desired that His people have a choice between good and evil, the unsaved won't be robots without volition. Millennial children born among the unsaved populace will never have known anything other than its "hothouse" spiritual climate. God will test each of them for obedience and allegiance before He will allow them to enter the golden eternity that follows.

Back in Moses' day, he challenged all the people: **I have set before thee this day life and good, and death and evil** (Deuteronomy 30:15). At some stage, millennial children will each have to make their own choice. God will make certain none enters the final age that harbors the potential for spiritual rebellion. The short season of Satan's loosing at the end of the Millennium will allow one last screening of all humanity. Each will get one last chance to choose good or evil. This will be the time of final exams before our graduation into eternity!

This choice of life or death has been going on since the beginning. Until they could be tested, Adam and Eve were denied access to the incredible tree of life. With an assist from the serpent, they blew it and were ejected from Eden lest they eat of that eternal-life tree. God knew that as a consequence of the fall, they would grow more and more evil. Thus God dare not permit them to live forever. Otherwise through the centuries, they would have developed into grotesque, reprobate beings.

In the Millennium, I believe Christians who have passed this same test and chosen life through Jesus *will* be invited to eat of that same great tree. Jesus said, **To him that overcometh will I give to eat of the tree of life, which is in the midst of the paradise of God** (Revelation 2:7).

When we are raptured, every physical flaw and sickness will go, "Poof!" **Then the eyes of the blind shall be opened, and the ears of the deaf shall be unstopped** (Isaiah 35:5).

141

We will be touched instantaneously, both mentally and physically. Our loving heavenly Father will erase all flaws resulting from sin, environment, and heredity. Paul says of our new body,

> *It is sown in corruption; it is raised in incorruption:*
> *It is sown in dishonour; it is raised in glory: it is sown*
> *in weakness; it is raised in power.* *1 Corinthians 15:42-43*

The design of humankind is the most luxurious in all of God's creation. We're the Rolls Royce of His universe. Only people bear the divine stamp "Made in Our Image" since God fashioned us to have the character qualities of the Father, the Son, and the Holy Spirit. At translation, we will become what God originally intended. And that's important, since we will live in our new state forever and forever. Paul tells the Christian to look forward to this time, to Jesus,

> *Who shall change our vile body, that it may be*
> *fashioned like unto his glorious body.* *Philippians 3:21*

Each believer, a perfect and unique individual in the family of God, will, at last, reach full stature and beauty as a one-of-a-kind person. The variety in all His creation exceeds human conception. Every snowflake, every fingerprint, and every person is different. God has no duplicates, no redundancy. He has but one *you* in His inventory. No wonder He has gone to such extreme measures to redeem each person.

So it won't be long now until you can meet the person Jesus intended you to be. In a twinkling of an eye, He will recast you into the perfect, original design He worked out for you before He fashioned the world. Remember, **He hath chosen us in him before the foundation of the world** (Ephesians 1:4). And God never designed a homely, crippled, or blemished person. He doesn't even know how to make "seconds." Each Millennium saint will be perfect and strikingly beautiful!

INSTANT YOUTH

Have you ever looked at a group of senior citizens and tried to imagine what they looked like when they were younger? Won't it be fun, in the Millennium, to see some of the lovely young people we've always thought of as old? Yes, Millennium saints will be vivacious and handsome!

> *When he comes back he will take these*
> *dying bodies of ours and change them into*
> *glorious bodies like his own.* Philippians 3:21 TLB

It seems almost too good to be true, doesn't it? Since this is now approaching "current event" status, it might be profitable to look at it a bit closer.

At some coming microsecond of time, glorified saints will find themselves far better than in their finest prime years— pulsing with beauty, vitality, and freshness! We will, however, still carry into glorification the accumulation of character that we have developed.

Everything bad will be left behind. God didn't craft physical imperfections. Instead the accumulation of thousands of years of human sin made them. These flaws, therefore, won't be brought into the immortalized being. The re-creation of millions seems a formidable task to our limited human minds, but it is a mere trifle to the God who spoke the worlds into existence and created something out of nothing. God will re-create us to His divine specifications.

A THOUSAND YEARS YOUNG

The built-in capacity of the human body to replace its own cells may hint at Millennium's eternal-youth capability. Most cells of our body can replace themselves when damaged or worn out. It seems reasonable that this automatic cellular replacement will be perfected in the Millennium, so that a thousand-year-old man could easily retain the glow of youth. There would be a continual renewing of our every cell.

The Lord has, at times, even caused inanimate objects to retain their newness. During the children of Israel's 40-year desert trek, God made sure that their clothing and shoes never wore out. This is an exciting picture of God's capacity to keep our person eternally shiny, new, and vibrant! Surely He can do for our bodies what He has already done with inanimate shoes. Now we can see why there is no need to fret about aging or physical imperfections. They trouble us only temporarily. And we'll want that eternal vitality. There are a billion galaxies to visit and a lot of forever to enjoy.

CHAPTER 18

A PLANT OF RENOWN

And I will raise up for them a plant of renown,
and they shall be no more consumed
with hunger in the land. *Ezekiel 34:29*

Would it startle you to realize that during the Millennium farmers will grow crops, ranchers will raise cattle, and they'll do so without having to fight the earth and the devouring insects? Here again, we've had such a hazy understanding of millennial life that we may not have considered the necessity of food production. Some of our traditional concepts of the Millennium have such an ethereal aura that we just haven't put much thought to practical basics such as eating, housing, and transportation. But through millennial scriptures these realities are slowly coming into focus. Paul speaks of our gradual understanding of God's plan:

*Now we see through a glass, darkly; but then face
to face: now I know in part; but then shall I know
even as also I am known.* 1 Corinthians 13:12

God wants us to peer through that murky glass and take strength from the glories we see.

Make no mistake, during the Millennium we'll hear the sounds of hammering, sawing, and the whir of the planter:

*And they shall build houses, and inhabit them; and
they shall plant vineyards, and eat the fruit of them.
They shall not build, and another inhabit .
They shall not labour in vain.* Isaiah 65:21-23

Through Ezekiel's prophetic pen, we see we **shall build houses, and plant vineyards; yea, they shall dwell with confidence** (Ezekiel 28:26). Can you see the emerald-green fields dotted with fabulous millennial buildings? The fields exploding with lush millennial flowers, fruit, and grain? The birds, frolicking animals, butterflies, and contented people?

THE LION TAMER

On the day God lifts His curse on the earth, He's going to make a total change in the animal kingdom. He will do as He said,

*And I will make with them a covenant of peace, and will cause
the evil beasts to cease out of the land: and they shall dwell
safely in the wilderness, and sleep in the woods.* Ezekiel 34:25

Again God speaks of this through the prophet Hosea:

And in that day will I make a covenant *for them
with the beasts of the field and with the fowls of heaven,
and with the creeping things of the ground: and I will
break the bow and the sword and the battle out of the
earth, and will make them to lie down safely.* Hosea 2:18

He will personally covenant with the wild animals, changing
their present treacherous natures back to the way they were
created to be. In a way, they will be "born again" to harmonize
with the rest of millennial creation. As a direct result of God's
wild animal modifications, they will never again be carnivo-
rous. Since earth's curse, some animals have been flesh eaters.
Lions, wolves, bears, and others have long attacked men. When
they become vegetarians instead of people-eaters, we'll enjoy
their company more, won't we?

Joel wrote about the wonderful blessings coming to the
"reformed" animals:

*Fear not, O land; be glad and rejoice:
for the Lord will do great things.
Be not afraid, ye beasts of the field: for the
pastures of the wilderness do spring.* Joel 2:21-22

Neither has God forgotten the cattle:

*I will feed them in a good pasture, and upon the high
mountains...there shall they lie in a good fold,
and in a fat pasture shall they feed.* Ezekiel 34:14

Isaiah speaks of the coming harmony among the animals
themselves:

*The wolf also shall dwell with the lamb,
and the leopard shall lie down with the kid....
And the cow and the bear shall feed...
and the lion shall eat straw like the ox.
They shall not hurt nor destroy.* Isaiah 11:6-7,9

It's going to be fun getting acquainted with all the birds and
animals. Man has a deep-down longing to be their friend.
That's why a trip to the zoo is so much fun. There's a special
thrill when we coax a bird or a squirrel to make friends even if
it's just a little sparrow enticed by crumbs on our windowsill.

Might this deep urge have come down from the Garden of
Eden? Adam lived among the animals and experienced joy in
that communion. He knew them so intimately the Lord
entrusted him to name each of them. That act has a profound
connotation. Restoration of man-animal relations will provide
a very bright corner in millennial life.

A PROPHET NAMED WALT

You know, I think we may have had an unrecognized
"prophet" at work. He was a very unusual kind of prophet

from a modern-day Gomorrah called Hollywood. Remember wonderful Walt Disney's cartoons with the little animals sitting around a campfire, swaying and clapping their hands, wagging their tails and singing? Perhaps those cartoons were prophetic. I think we may actually see that during the Millennium. The animals will even join in with us as we sing and praise the Lord. Can you hear it?

Let every thing that hath breath praise the Lord. Psalm 150:6

People, animals, trees, hills, and maybe even flowers will get in on the act. Wow—what a choir! I wonder what we'll do when a friendly millennial hippopotamus tries to sit on our lap?

LORD OF THE CRICKETS

But what about bugs? It's still hard to visualize a perfect environment that would include the stings of mosquitoes, hornets, bees, spiders, and flies, isn't it? Although prophecy doesn't specifically mention the insect world, if the Lord will tame the rattlesnake, I don't think we have to worry about buzzing gnats. The promise of Eden-like life certifies the elimination of insect trouble. I imagine they'll still be around to perform their functions in nature, but bugs just won't bug *us.* We'll be able to enjoy our evening lakeside picnics without a swarm of crawling and flying pests.

In fact, I believe the insect world will join us in praising God. Several years ago Pat Boone had a delightful foretaste of this coming harmony. Pat's eyes were wide when he told us what happened.

> I was staying with my parents for a few days while doing some recording in Nashville. Early one evening I was singing out on Mama's porch swing all by myself. Five or ten minutes after I started to sing out there, the presence of the Lord came down in a very unique way. The songs of praise rose higher in my throat as I was caught up in worship.
>
> Suddenly I became aware of some new voices chiming in—a great cricket chorus was joining in with me. It was so startling that I quit right in mid-song and—you guessed it—the crickets stopped too. Hesitantly I started to sing again, and once more that cricket choir joined right in on my praises.

THE GOOD EARTH

There's something deeply stirring about seeing magnificent fields of ripe grain and orchards of fruit-laden trees. Have you ever seen the acres of blossoming tulips in Holland? The explosion of luxuriant trees and foliage in the South Pacific islands is also breathtaking! Wild coconuts, bananas, and papayas seem like a foretaste of the Millennium. Sometimes I think God put those unspoiled islands out there to give us a hint of verdant eternity.

Yet agronomists say they are worried over the earth's approaching incapability to feed her passenger load. Increasingly we hear of famines caused by drought, pestilence, and over-population. So it would be quite understandable if some might wonder how this world could ever feed a huge millennial populace—including saints from all generations plus millions of non-glorified citizens.

Well, there will be plenty of people, but there will never again be any need for concern about shortages. That pale horse of the Apocalypse will be forever tied. The Scripture promises about Millennium food are magnificent! We will no longer suffer the consequences of the curse caused by Adam's sin. (See Genesis 3:17-19.) The restructured earth will, by then, have millions of newly fertile acres for farming. And farmers will especially appreciate the profound consequences of no more weeds, blight, or devouring insects. Under this present time of the earth's curse, these combine to destroy millions of tons of food.

Perfecting earth's climate will likewise multiply the quantity and enhance the quality of its food. No more drought, floods, hail, frosts, or damaging winds. Isaiah says,

> *Then shall he give the rain to thy seed, that thou shalt sow the ground withal; and the bread of the increase of the earth, and it shall be fat and plenteous.* Isaiah 30:23

Let's review just a few of the extraordinary passages about this millennial horn-of-plenty:

> *And I will multiply the fruit of the tree, and the increase of the field.* Ezekiel 36:30

*But they shall sit every man under
his vine and under his fig tree.* Micah 4:4

*So the Lord shall make bright clouds, and give them
showers of rain, to every one grass in the field.* Zechariah 10:1

And the desolate land shall be tilled. Ezekiel 36:34

*In that day shall the branch of the Lord be
beautiful and glorious, and the fruit of the
earth shall be excellent and comely.* Isaiah 4:2

*For the seed shall be prosperous; the vine shall give
her fruit, and the ground shall give her increase,
and the heavens shall give their dew.* Zechariah 8:12

*And the parched ground shall become a pool,
and the thirsty land springs of water.* Isaiah 35:7

FAIR AND WARMER

Not only will there be unprecedented fertility, but also no further seasonal time lapses between crops:

Behold, the days come, saith the Lord, that the plowman shall overtake the reaper, *and the treader of grapes him that soweth seed; and the mountains shall drop sweet wine.* Amos 9:13

Even today, by utilizing the technique of hydroponic farming, it's possible to grow more food in a small 40-by-180-foot plot than on ten acres of ground in the traditional way. Using such idealized agricultural methods, some remarkable products have already been grown, such as hundred-pound watermelons and eight-foot tomato plants with fruits that weigh a pound and a half! And millennial farmers will make these beauties look pretty ordinary.

What is that mysterious and exciting promise God made through Ezekiel?

> *And I will raise up for them a* plant of renown, *and they shall be no more consumed with hunger.* Ezekiel 34:29

Some Bible scholars interpret this plant of renown to be Jesus, the **tender plant, and...a root out of a dry ground** of Isaiah 53:2. But taken literally, we can ask, "Could God be fashioning a wonder plant for the Millennium? Might it have the combined flavor of strawberry, banana, mango, and orange?" I don't know, but I do know that **neither have it entered into the heart of man, the things which God hath prepared for them that love him** (1 Corinthians 2:9)! You can be sure that whatever God has in store for us will be exquisite, tasty, and remarkable. He is holding exciting things in store for us!

CHAPTER 19

SYMPHONIES IN STARDUST

No doubt the cherubs earn their wage who wind each ticking star. —Don Marquis

Out on distant planes of the universe, hidden by reefs of time and space, lie strange realms unlike anything in our wildest dreams. They crouch out there beyond reach of earth-bound man, bizarre and unexplored. But in recent years, gates into this cosmic realm have ever so slightly begun to crack open. Recent astrophysical breakthroughs are enabling mankind to catch their first glimpses of once-hidden galactic domains. These peeks have left heretofore unflappable scientists shaken. The more they learn, the more scrambled their notions about God, energies, and origins become.

Several years ago, *Time* magazine published a magnificent series of articles from their research on the deterioration in our present civilization. An excerpt from that series entitled *Second Thoughts About Man* says:

Man's confidence in his power to control his world is suddenly at a low ebb. The scientists themselves are now depressed to realize that their universe is far more complex than they recently thought and that they have fewer solutions than hoped.

What has shattered these scientists' serenity and smugness? Here's what: They've discovered that far out there in the wild, wonderful cosmos there are such things as:

- Mysterious black holes with gravity so strong light cannot escape

- Baffling tiny orbs, shining with the power of a trillion suns

- Stardust, cosmic rays, and collapsed stars wandering silently

- Million-mile-an-hour solar winds

- Stars singing, each with their own voices (see Job 38)

- Super novas like celestial fireworks

Yes, the heavens declare the glory of God, just as the Psalmist stated in Psalm 19. For eons God's finger has been inscribing a cosmic testimony. The writing in the heavenlies tells of mysteries with deep spiritual and practical relevance to every believer. Let's examine a few of God's celestial wonders.

Quasars are small, jewel-like bodies packed with more energy then ten entire galaxies the size of our own. In one minute some quasars emit enough power to supply all of the earth's needs for fifty million years.

Supernovae are the most dramatic of cosmic fireworks! Exploding stars spread gas clouds, meteoric fragments, and dust over millions of space miles. These fiery displays are so grandiose they can be watched for hundreds of years.

Pulsars are neutron stars spinning at enormous speeds that somehow emit their signals in pulses. Pulsars are so dense that one thimbleful of a pulsar weighs more than 50,000 locomotives.

Physicists are staggered by mounting evidence of the universe's size. Astrophysical devices are now bringing in breathtaking new information about deep space. If Galileo could see the present array of instruments available to modern-day astrophysicists, he would turn green with envy:

- The Hubble space telescope
- The huge 200-inch Mt. Palomar optical telescope
- Radio telescopes like Aricibo in Puerto Rico
- Instrumented spacecraft like Voyager, Surveyor, and Mars Pathfinder

What magnificent tools! But what is causing some to gasp as the data rolls in? For one thing they are just beginning to fathom the scope of the universe.

We are now cruising along at a cool 66,000 miles an hour, orbiting the sun on a planet which poet Archibald MacLeish described as "a small planet...of a minor star...off at the edge of an inconsiderable galaxy." On this small planet, scientists labor feverishly to prove Rene Descartes' proclamation true. The haughty philosopher bragged: "There is nothing so far removed from us as to be beyond our reach; or so hidden that we cannot discover it."

But the Bible speaks of men such as Descartes, saying **the mouth of fools poureth out foolishness** (Proverbs 15:2), and God always has the final word. Instead of providing an answer, this new torrent of cosmic data leaves scientists ever more baffled. Physicists listen today with new awe as their own instruments whisper of the universe's scope.

We've learned that gigantic heavenly galaxies are as common as grains of sand on a beach. There are a billion of them! No wonder confusion is king among some in the intellectual community. It's about time men listen to what those stars are trying to tell them about their Creator. But don't hold your breath because even to the keenest natural mind these secrets will only breed still more controversy. The Bible says,

None of the wicked shall understand. Daniel 12:10

Until time itself ends, those who trust exclusively in their own understanding will stay confused. They will generate more and more vain theories as long as they ignore the Bible— which is, among other things, an accurate book of science. Let's look a bit at their confusion. Nobel Prize winner George Wald once wrote, "I think there is no question in that we live in an inhabited universe that has life all over it." Wald has a lot of distinguished company who concur with this position.

Yet others with equal scientific credentials insist, "There's not a shred of evidence that there is life out there in space."

Yes, the non-spiritual community is in disarray, and it's not just concerning life on other planets. They're also confused concerning the origin of the universe. For instance, hundreds of eminent physicists hold to a steady-state universe theory, while hundreds more cling to the "Big Bang" theory. These latter scholars presume that, many eons ago, the universe was in one big ball until a cataclysmic explosion occurred! They claim that, as a result, the whole universe is rushing outward at fantastic speed. In time, they theorize, all this matter will implode. Everything will begin reversing direction and racing back into one dense mass—only to repeat the whole process, time and again, like some bouncing ball.

What a bizarre explanation! I wonder if anyone ever asked them, "Who put the mass of matter out there in the first place, and who lit the fuse?" You can be glad if this "Big Bang" theory seems ridiculous to you. "In the beginning God..." is a much more logical conclusion. There is a special kind of wisdom among believers that operates *above* the intellectual plane. Jesus described it this way,

> *It is given unto you to know the mysteries of the kingdom of heaven, but to them* (the carnal and unbelieving) *it is not given. Matthew 13:11*

Yes, the Bible has a better idea:

> *The Lord by wisdom hath founded the earth; by understanding hath he established the heavens. Proverbs 3:19*

If a man does not keep pace with his companions,
perhaps it is because he hears a different drummer.
Let him step to the music he hears, however
measured or far away. —Henry David Thoreau

Those who wrote the Bible and those who live by its truths
hear and believe only the music of the Holy Drummer!

Chapter 20

Cosmic Thunder

Yes, the cosmos is grudgingly opening her secrets. Will we ever detect the edge of the universe? Well, we're certainly trying. Since its launch in 1990, the Hubble space telescope has provided remarkable new views of the universe which have revolutionized astronomers' thinking about many astronomical mysteries. Hubble's powerful capabilities have allowed astronomers to peer into the outer limits of the universe and uncover a variety of never-before-seen galaxies. Astronomers always hoped it would enable them to view the very edge of the universe. I predict that ultimately they'll be disappointed. Our God and His universe are beyond measuring with the puny instruments of men, as He revealed to Job:

> *Where wast thou when I laid the foundations of*
> *the earth? declare, if thou hast understanding....*
> *Knowest thou the ordinances of heaven? canst thou*
> *set the dominion thereof in the earth?* Job 38:4,33

God's creation continues to boggle the puny scientific mind. Early in 1999, the Hubble space telescope's imaging spectrograph recorded the most powerful cosmic explosion recorded to date. For a brief moment the light from the blast was equal to the radiance of *one hundred million billion* stars! While scientists are still scratching their heads, I can tell you what caused it: God did it!

Yes, the works of God are too colossal! How can mortal man ever expect to plumb infinity? While we applaud the magnificent achievements of the scholars and scientists, some of their feverish efforts to disprove God remind me of the Shakespearean character in Hamlet who said, "The lady doth protest too much, methinks."

God has forthrightly declared the origin of life, and yet many extend to the limits of lunacy their efforts to tread down God's explanation. The Bible tells us that **great men are not always wise** (Job 32:9). The contortions some scholars put themselves through to disprove God's Word border on the humorous. They struggle through tortured theories to discount the Bible. Paul describes them as among those **who changed the truth of God into a lie** (Romans 1:25).

Many who are otherwise intelligent have psyched themselves into believing things like this bizarre theory of man's origin: "Three and one-half billion years ago a violent celestial storm broke. Thunder, lightning, and solar radiation stirred a primordial soup. Out of this came amino acids, and from the brew, life forms began to invent themselves."

Can't you just see those little amino-acid molecules running around until they accidentally "self-invent" an optical system, a heart, a brain, and love! Methinks they protest against God too much! It takes more faith to believe that silliness than it does to believe the Bible. And it doesn't require a towering intellect to recognize intellectual confusion:

> *Thus saith the Lord, thy redeemer, and he that formed*
> *thee from the womb, I am the Lord that maketh*
> *all things; that stretcheth forth the heavens alone;*
> *that spreadeth abroad the earth by myself;*
>
> *That frustrateth the tokens of the liars, and*
> *maketh diviners mad; that turneth wise men backward,*
> *and maketh their knowledge foolish.* Isaiah 44:24-25

Plato wrote, "Astronomy compels the soul to look upward." The grandeur, variety, and magnitude of the celestial menagerie excites my passion for God:

> *For as the heavens are higher than the earth,*
> *so are my ways higher than your ways, and*
> *my thoughts than your thoughts.* Isaiah 55:9

The sheer *size* of creation shorts out human comprehension! A light beam speeding 186,000 miles every second takes 1,000 years just to cross our own galaxy. And by now we know more than a billion other galaxies exist, so it shouldn't be surprising that God has fashioned some exotic cosmic mysteries. Each discovery of one of His creations makes Him seem still grander and more glorious to me.

Those black holes in our universe fascinate us. They exert such massive pull that everything within a million miles is sucked inside to be forever trapped. Some astronomers theorize that at one time they were huge bodies that have undergone gravitational collapse. Compressed to such density, their gravity warps space and time which fold in on each other. But black holes are so mysterious no one really understands them.

Since their enormous pull prevents even light from escaping, they can only be detected by X-ray. Dr. Thorne of the California Institute of Technology says, "We will never be able to see inside a black hole, and we can never know what has happened inside, since no energy, in any form, ever comes out to carry the information."

By using Hubble to measure the whirlpool-like motion of stars and gas in the cores of galaxies, astronomers have calculated how much matter is packed into a galaxy's hub. In the three galaxies the space telescope has probed so far, scientists have calculated that the mass of hundreds of millions or billions of suns is compressed into a region of space no bigger than our solar system...they think.

Strange indeed! Could it be some of these black holes out in space may prove to be places for being consigned to outer darkness? Could one of them be the bottomless pit? No one knows. Maybe when we attend Jesus University, we can find out their real purpose in God's universal economy.

But black holes aren't the real mystery in space. Somewhere out there is a dazzling opposite to the outer darkness. It is the most beautiful territory in the universe, according to those Bible heroes who have seen it—the apostle Paul and John the Revelator, for example. Lavish with priceless stones, gold, and crystal, it's the control center for everything that is. It's God's office and His residence.

Is not God in the height of heaven? and behold
the height of the stars, how high they are! Job 22:12

We will be staying there with Jesus during the tribulation years, and it would be heartbreaking to leave if we weren't returning to earth with the One who carries heaven with Him—Jesus, the Son.

FASTEN YOUR SEAT BELT

Some years ago I was studying a group of scriptures that reveal our relationship with the rest of creation. The heavenly Father states flatly that all things in heaven and in earth are put under Jesus. Then we are told,

We are the children of God.
Then heirs; heirs of God, and
joint-heirs with Christ. Romans 8:16-17

For still further confirmation we read in Psalm 8:3-4,6:

*When I consider thy heavens, the work
of thy fingers, the moon and the stars;...
What is man, that thou art mindful of him?...
Thou madest him to have dominion over the works
of thy hands: thou hast put all things under his feet.*

This exciting passage of Scripture is repeated in the New Testament in Hebrews 2. And there came that moment when suddenly the implications of that message exploded within me! The Lord is clearly telling about our own eternal involvement with His entire universe. We must stretch our vision to encompass our millennial assignments in God's colossal realms during eternity.

This started me thinking of some logistical problems such travel would present. I said, "Lord, it will take too long to get out there to the far reaches of Your space. Even at the blinding speed of light it takes a thousand years to cross our own little galaxy. Since You created at least a billion more, it would consume my eternity just to travel out there on assignments. How could this problem ever be solved?"

Within seconds a question entered my mind. "What is the fastest thing you can think of in all the universe?"

As I was pondering this, I thought of lightning, the speed of comets, and light at 186,000 miles a second. I said, "Light is the fastest."

Then I got another mental nudge. "No, light is too slow. Keep thinking."

Finally it struck. Why of course, there is something faster—the speed of *thought!* Remember, we will have the unhindered mind of Christ in our glorified bodies. Suddenly I saw how it would be possible for us to fulfill our millennial assignments anywhere. Wow! We'll just have to *think there* to *be there!*

Imagine the might and power of our Creator to adorn the universe with a trillion massive planets, stars, and celestial mysteries. He who with incomparable divinity has hung it all on nothing.

> *He stretcheth out the north over the empty place, and hangeth the earth upon nothing....*
> *The pillars of heaven tremble and are astonished at his reproof....*
> *By his spirit he hath garnished the heavens...*
> *Lo, these are parts of his ways: but how little a portion is heard of him? but the thunder of his power who can understand?* Job 26:7,11,13-14

Just think: We imagine what the universe must be like, but God tells us clearly that we don't know the half of it!

CHAPTER 21

INVASION OF THE OVERCOMERS

At the peak of the fury of the Battle of Armageddon, the warriors will be suddenly awestruck at the most dramatic sight earthlings have ever seen. They will stare skyward at this sight, which will render the most bizarre science fiction ever written dull and pale. Listen to the apostle John's description of it:

> *And I saw heaven opened, and behold a white horse;*
> *and he that sat upon him was called Faithful and True....*
> *His eyes were as a flame of fire,*
> *and on his head were many crowns....*
> *And he was clothed with a vesture dipped in*
> *blood: and his name is called The Word of God.*
> *And the armies which were in heaven followed him*
> *upon white horses, clothed in fine linen, white and clean.*
> *And he hath on his vesture and on his thigh a name written,*
> KING, OF KINGS, AND LORD OF LORDS. *Revelation 19:11-14,16*

This spine-tingling invasion from outer space will be made up of a colossal army of the redeemed, spiritual "good guys" who back up their Commander, Jesus Christ. Baseball great Leo Durocher coined a slogan, "Good guys finish last." But as this big army invades earth it will forever disprove Leo's catchy nonsense about the good guys. The world has portrayed believers as flakes and losers for too long. Jesus and His returning saints will be living proof that, in the end, Christians are big, big winners!

This world will never truly be compatible with the believer until it is seized by these heavenly forces and made habitable for the righteous. This place can't really be our home until Jesus "fumigates" it of sin. God issued a basic command, ordering humankind to subdue and replenish the earth. Adam was ordered to take dominion. But even before the Millennium, God still expects us to be stewards of earth's physical resources, as well as our spiritual treasures. This has never changed, even though Satan is still prince of this world. We have been commissioned to occupy until Jesus returns.

We should be spiritual occupiers and commandos. It isn't enough for us to receive God's gift of salvation and then just relax or hide out until Jesus returns. After salvation, He expects us to learn His principles of spiritual warfare and then apply them. We are being trained in this life to exercise stewardship over all God provides for us: possessions, time, and talents. (See Luke 16.) And He expects believers to develop a "can-do" spiritual posture. The believer should be a warrior on the attack—constantly taking new ground.

The Lord watches and tests us in this life, which He shared in a revealing parable about a certain nobleman who went away to receive a kingdom in Luke 19:12-27. Each of the servants was entrusted with one pound and told, **Occupy till I come** (Luke 19:13). The pound represents the time, money, talents, and spiritual opportunities each believer encounters during this lifetime.

When the nobleman returned, each of the servants (representing us) was called before him. The first servant said, "Lord, your pound has gained ten pounds."

The master said, "Well done, good servant. Because you have been faithful in a very little, I give you authority over ten cities." Another servant gained five pounds, and was rewarded with authority over five cities.

But one servant foolishly hid his pound. He was like the Christian who receives salvation and then just sits on his spiritual potential. The master was anything but pleased and ordered the unused pound to be seized and given to the servant who had been so aggressive and profitable with the master's provision.

It seems clear from Jesus' parable that our spiritual performance in this life determines our reigning position during the kingdom age. He wants us to do whatever we can for the kingdom with whatever we have.

EXCELLENT POSITIONS AVAILABLE

There will be high management openings for can-do Christians during millennial civilization. Jesus is now quietly recruiting those demonstrating capability as overcomers. He needs saints who develop success patterns in this present, real-life testing ground through their application of His spiritual principles.

The Lord has published His spiritual principles in a valuable "how-to" manual. It's called the Bible! By practicing its spiritual formulas, we can be converted from chronic losers into consistent winners.

That ye would walk worthy of God, who hath called
you unto his kingdom and glory. 1 Thessalonians 2:12

Many leaders will be needed to reign over cities, regions, nations, territories and special millennial projects. Even if we don't realize it, we are now training for these kingdom age assignments:

Let a man so account of us, as...
stewards of the mysteries of God.
Moreover it is required in stewards, that
a man be found faithful. 1 Corinthians 4:1-2

And don't be surprised when we find some little-known Christians reigning in positions of great honor and scope during the kingdom age. We may remember some as "little" people who humbly labored for the Lord in low-profile positions He assigned them. But God marks those who learn to properly wield the weapons of spiritual victory. The Bible says,

> *The weapons of our warfare are not carnal,*
> *but mighty through God to the pulling*
> *down of strong holds.* 2 Corinthians 10:4

We are in mortal combat with unseen forces and the stakes in this battle are eternal:

> *We wrestle not against flesh and blood, but against principalities,*
> *against powers, against the rulers of the darkness of this world,*
> *against spiritual wickedness in high places.* Ephesians 6:12

To fully prepare for our role in Jesus Christ's invading army, we must work to develop our skills with the spiritual weapons and armor described in Ephesians 6. Jesus paid a price so that we who believe might be mighty warriors in Him:

> *They overcame him by the blood of the Lamb,*
> *and by the word of their testimony.* Revelation 12:11

To be sure, leadership in this battle is a matter of choice. We can run and hide, or we can do our part. Neither heavenly crowns nor millennial positions will be given to the fearful and unbelieving. God designed us to wield such power so that the gates of hell would not prevail against us. (See Matthew 16:18.) We are being groomed to assume leadership roles in His universe by learning spiritual disciplines.

Olympic champions must not only have talent, they must exercise great daily discipline in order to become winners. Those who are slack in their daily discipline will not win any prizes. But the prizes for disciplined believers are dazzling. In Revelation, God showcases a display of those glittering spiritual trophies soon to be awarded to Christians who let the Holy Spirit develop them into overcomers. Here is a partial array of God's prizes for the overcomer:

> *To him that overcometh will I give to* eat
> of the tree of life, *which is in the midst*
> *of the paradise of God.* Revelation 2:7

> *To him that overcometh will I give to*
> *eat of the* hidden manna. Revelation 2:17

> *And to he that overcometh, and keepeth my works*
> *unto the end, to him will I give* power over the nations...
> *And I will give him* the morning star. Revelation 2:26, 28

> *He that overcometh, the same shall be clothed in*
> white raiment; *and I will not blot out his name out*
> *of the book of life, but I* will confess his name *before*
> *my Father, and before his angels.* Revelation 3:5

> *Him that overcometh will I* make a pillar
> *in the temple of my God.* Revelation 3:12

> *To him that overcometh will I grant to* sit
> with me in my throne, *even as I also overcame, and*
> *am set down with my Father in his throne.* Revelation 3:21

*He that overcometh shall inherit all things; and I
will be his God, and he shall be my son.* Revelation 21:7

Will you be an overcomer? God is now training His children
for victory under the tutelage of the Holy Spirit. For us to
develop overcoming skills, we must develop spiritual understanding and maintain great discipline. It also takes consistent
practice in real-life situations. Every day. But as the previous
scriptures illustrate, the rewards will be beyond our imagination.

CHAPTER 22

A BRIGHT GOLDEN HAZE

One of the prominent facets of life in the Millennium is also one of the most elusive aspects for us to understand: *The glory of God will fill the earth!* I just wonder if, during our present state, we can ever really grasp this colossal millennial truth?

> *And the glory of the Lord shall be revealed,*
> *and all flesh shall see it together.* Isaiah 40:5
>
> *Blessed be his glorious name for ever: and let the*
> *whole earth be filled with his glory.* Psalm 72:19

The Bible records instances down through time when the glory and presence of divinity were briefly exposed:

> *Then I beheld, and lo a likeness as the appearance of fire:*
> *from the appearance of his loins even downward, fire;*
> *and from his loins even upward, as the appearance*
> *of brightness, as the colour of amber.* Ezekiel 8:2

These visitations often resulted in a shattering emotional experience for the humans witnessing them. People fell on their faces in fear when an angel, a mere *messenger* of God, appeared!

The glory will blind enemy soldiers and horses during earth's climactic battle:

> *In that day, saith the Lord, I will smite every horse*
> (of the armies that contend against Jerusalem) *with astonishment, and his rider with madness: and I will open mine eyes upon the house of Judah, and will smite every horse of the people with blindness.* Zechariah 12:4

Human beings, in their present state, can't tolerate proximity to this glory. In Exodus 3 Moses once saw God's glory as a burning bush. At other times, in Exodus 13, His glory appeared as a cloud by day and a pillar of fire by night. When the ark of the covenant was foolishly opened, thousands perished through exposure to the presence of God. (See 1 Samuel 6.)

When Moses came down from that mountain meeting with God, his being was charged with radiated glory. Just from Moses' nearness to it, his face had to be veiled because of an unbearable incandescence. And the glory immobilized the Jews when it filled the traveling tabernacle:

> *And it came to pass, when the priests were come out of the holy place, that the cloud filled the house of the Lord,*
>
> *So that the priests could not stand to minister because of the cloud: for the glory of the Lord had filled the house.* 1 Kings 8:10-11

In the New Testament, Peter wanted to build three monuments when Jesus appeared in His glorified state with Moses and Elijah on the Mount of Transfiguration. (See Matthew 17.) The glory seems to blow fuses in our present emotional network! Quite often contact with the glory caused Bible personalities to faint from awe or fear. On the road to Damascus, Paul was left blinded and trembling from the light from heaven and the voice of Jesus. (See Acts 9.)

After we are remanufactured at the resurrection, our bodies will then be capable of rejoicing in the literal presence of His glory. That glory can destroy the wicked but causes the righteous to rejoice:

> *Lift up your heads, O ye gates; even lift them up,*
> *ye everlasting doors; and the King of glory shall come in.*
> *Who is this King of glory? The Lord of hosts,*
> *he is the King of glory.* Psalm 24:9-10

The Bible tells us that God displays certain of His glories for our benefit:

> *The heavens declare the glory of God; and the*
> *firmament sheweth his handywork.* Psalm 19:1

Throughout nature we find hints of His glory like road signs pointing toward the full-voltage millennial presence of God. Let's look at a few of these signs we now experience in rare moments and then imagine these amplified during every millennial hour—never again to be just fleeting thrills. Now we get tiny hints, like morning sunshine on a tiny flower, the sight of a rainbow during an incredible sunset, the smell of springtime with the sound of a bird's song, and the sound of rolling thunder and warm summer rain. In the Millennium, these will no longer be the unusual, the exception, but the norm. The Bible says,

> *He shall come down like rain upon the mown grass:*
> *as showers that water the earth.* Psalm 72:6

When His glory comes to stay, it will bring an ecstasy so intense that we will need to have glorified bodies just to survive. Think of it, the *glory of God filling the earth!* Are you ready for that?

> *When the Son of man shall come in his glory,*
> *and all the holy angels with him, then shall*
> *he sit upon the throne of his glory.* Matthew 25:31

This bright golden haze of the Lord's presence will bring an indescribable sense of well-being. No wonder the Millennium will be punctuated with laughter, praise, and dancing! When Jesus came to earth for those thirty-three incredible years, He did mighty works and His glory was present wherever He was. In the Millennium His glory won't be confined to the spot where He stands. In that day His glory will permeate the entire planet!

THE SINGING HILLS

For God is the King of all the earth: sing ye
praises with understanding. Psalm 47:7

We've all felt a mysterious rousing of expectancy when we sing the song *The King Is Coming.* If just our anticipation can excite such a great emotional charge, imagine the wallop we will experience when we sing, *The King Is Here!*

Have you secretly wondered if it might get a little boring having so much praise time after we are with the Lord? There is nothing more dominant in millennial prophecy than its record of explosive, reverberating enthusiasm for praise! Believe me, the Millennium is going to be gloriously noisy! Our reserved emotions will melt, and we will break into full-throated adoration. Those of us who can't carry a tune will delight in our new millennial voices. There will be laughter, twirling people, clapping hands, and loud hosannas!

Some of us staid Christians will have to abandon our wooden concept of worship. We have rationalized our spiritual inhibitions by saying we want to "do things decently and in order." But the Bible tells us,

Then shall the virgin rejoice in the dance,
both young men and old together: for I will
turn their mourning into joy. Jeremiah 31:13

That doesn't sound too solemn and pompous. Enthusiastic worship neither embarrasses nor makes the Lord nervous as it does some people. In fact, everything in creation cuts loose! The stars, the ground, the sea, the fields, and the trees will erupt in praise.

> *Let the heavens rejoice, and let the earth*
> *be glad; let the sea roar....*
> *Let the field be joyful....*
> *Then shall all the trees of the wood rejoice.*
> *Before the Lord.* Psalm 96:11-13

What happens when rock stars come to town? Pandemonium, shrieks, torn clothing, and even destruction—that's what happens. Emotional madness descends, which I believe is a demonic counterfeit of the coming praise and worship of the Lord. Some shrug their shoulders at the sick frenzies at rock concerts, yet these same people are horrified if someone says "Amen" out loud in Sunday service.

Watch the crowd at a football game. People really let their emotions take off when the home team scores. We jump to our feet, flail our arms and scream. Don't worry about the drink we spilled down that fellow's neck—*we won!* A bit of madness? Not necessarily. It's just human emotion being released for a few seconds—but for a far lesser occasion than the coming of the King.

Have you ever watched children run and leap when Daddy comes home after a trip? Kids hopping and shouting before the Christmas tree? The enthusiastic embrace when lovers meet? Sure you have. But they're just transitory thrills, like fragile bubbles of joy, which we enjoy during this lifetime. Soon these surges of delight won't be fleeting exceptions but a permanent state.

Do you wonder about the reason for the high level of millennial emotions? The answer lies in glorious presence of our Bridegroom. At every glance from Jesus, our passions will peak. Look at these passages from the Song of Solomon that prophetically describe the attraction between us, the bride, and Jesus, the Bridegroom:

For thy love is better than wine.... The flowers appear on the earth; the time of the singing of the birds is come.
My beloved is mine, and I am his....
Thy lips are like a thread of scarlet, and thy speech is comely....
Until the day break, and the shadows flee away,
I will get me to the mountain of myrrh, and to the
hill of frankincense. Song of Solomon 1:2, 2:12,16;4:3,6

Thou art all fair, my love....
Thou hast ravished my heart...How fair is thy love...
how much better is thy love than wine! Thy lips...
drop as the honeycomb: honey and milk are
under thy tongue; and the smell of thy garments is like
the smell of Lebanon. Song of Solomon 4:7, 9-11

My beloved is white and ruddy, the chiefest
among ten thousand. His head is as the most
fine gold, his locks are bushy, and black as a raven.

His eyes are as the eyes of doves....

His cheeks are as a bed of spices, as sweet flowers:
his lips like lilies, dropping sweet smelling myrrh...
His legs are as pillars of marble, set upon sockets of fine gold:
his countenance is as Lebanon, excellent as the cedars.
His mouth is most sweet: yea, he is altogether lovely.
This is my beloved.... Song of Solomon 5:10-16

How intimate is this revelation of our own millennial relationship with our glorious Bridegroom! If this promise doesn't set your heart to racing, then I dare you to read it again! No wonder everything comes "unglued" with joy in the Millennium!

For ye shall go out with joy, and be led forth with peace:
the mountains and the hills shall break forth before
you into singing, and all the trees of the field
shall clap their hands. Isaiah 55:12

How could the hills not sing and the trees not clap? How could our feet do anything but dance and the little animals do anything but leap at the very sight of Him!

The wilderness and the solitary place shall be glad for
them; and the desert shall rejoice, and blossom as the rose.
It shall blossom abundantly, and rejoice
even with joy and singing. Isaiah 35:1-2

But how long can such mighty ecstasy last? It will be unending:

Therefore shall the people praise
thee for ever and ever. Psalm 45:17

But be ye glad and rejoice for ever in that which I create....
And the voice of weeping shall be no more heard
in her, nor the voice of crying. Isaiah 65:18-19

Oh no, the love affair between Jesus and His bride won't be some transitory romance. It will blossom and soar as our understanding and our capacities are enlarged. It will take us centuries to fathom His glorious delights. The fragrance and intensity of our love will spiral higher through all the ages of His glory to come.

CHAPTER 23

SUPERWORLD!

As we make the transition into the twenty-first century, we've been seeing the deadliest, stormiest, and most despairing years in all history. But look! There's a cloud forming on the horizon, but this time it's a silver one! This planet is headed for glorious times, and all the king's horses and all the devil's angels can't stop it. The King of Kings is coming soon as vindicator of His Word and vindicator of His people.

Behold, one like the Son of man
came with the clouds of heaven....

And there was given him dominion, and glory,
and a kingdom, that all people, nations, and languages,
should serve him: his dominion is an everlasting dominion,
which shall not pass away, and his kingdom that
which shall not be destroyed. Daniel 7:13-14

For endless centuries men have dreamed of creating an ideal world—a Shangri-La. First came the Babylonians, then the Egyptians, the Greeks, and the Romans. They were followed in more recent times by the British, the Nazis, the Communists, and even the Americans. Each moved forward with a frenetic drive to usher in its own brand of global utopia. But one after another has ended in dust, smoke, slavery, or political disasters!

There are some jarring ruts still ahead as humanity's road stretches toward that silver millennial horizon. Today the world convulses from a terminal case of sin fever. Nevertheless, something big is in the air, and even a fool can sense the game is about up.

Masses grope for either salvation or suicide. Others try to drown their despair with alcohol. Here's why: In decades past, orators could weave a compelling tapestry which predicted a glowing future for mankind. "Soaring education and sky-rocketing technology," they said, "will bring a chicken in every pot, two cars in every garage, unheard of prosperity—can't you see it just ahead?"

But that promised future finally arrived, and instead of being the glittering one promised, it was leaden. The orators' golden horizons have turned ominously dark. A perplexed world stands leaderless and faint. The Bible warns against just such uncertainty:

Where there is no vision, the people perish. Proverbs 29:18

And so in the dusk of a dying age that newly forming silver cloud shines in the distance! We must herald the Good News of the reality of the Millennium with Jesus at its helm. We must tell of the very Superworld that has eluded civilization while man has been at the wheel.

We must bring its nearness into focus—just look at it! It has a rich vibrancy, rest, peace, dancing, and laughter. I can see the Millennium through that colossal door which is slowly, irreversibly, swinging shut. Jesus himself is the door and He's calling to the people on the dying planet: "I offer life abundant and eternal! Hurry! Don't waste precious time looking for another way into the kingdom. I am the only way. Come, the Millennium bells are ringing!"

Believers must sound the very Good News that the way is still open. Compel the world to safety before the door closes. It's an hour to let the Holy Spirit ignite one last spiritual revolution! The fire of the early Church must be kindled! Early Christians weren't ashamed to be counted with their leader to the point of death. Their Spirit-inspired zeal turned the world upside down! If first-century Christians died to tell others about Jesus the Savior, won't we at least risk embarrassment for Him?

Living on planet earth today is like being on the Titanic after it hit the iceberg, and it's time to tell a sinking world where to find Jesus, the Lifeboat. Let's go public with the news of Jesus' kingdom!

You can be sure that people will mock you for speaking the truth. But they won't mock long. Soon the swingers and the do-your-own-thingers will discover, one heartbeat too late, that Jesus isn't the emaciated, effeminate, pitiful, dead figure on the crucifix. Their laughter will freeze as they face a blazing-eyed, omnipotent, brilliant, authoritative, living Jesus.

And I will not let them pollute
my holy name any more. Ezekiel 39:7

It's time to go radical for righteousness—to declare war against sin and Satan—to rock the boat for Jesus! Never again are we to be timid about our allegiance to the One who hung the stars in space. We're His authorized representatives, His agents on this planet. Let our blood run hot against sin. The prophet Isaiah said,

I will not rest, until the righteousness
thereof go forth as brightness, and the
salvation thereof as a lamp burneth. Isaiah 62:1

Time to sound the final alert! Planet earth is about to be reborn!

The kingdoms of this world are become the kingdoms of our
Lord...and he shall reign for ever and ever. Revelation 11:15

Hosannas to the Father, to the Son, and to the Holy Ghost!

Look up! Those early streaks in the eastern sky herald the Millennium's dawn—a romantic, 1,000-year valentine from a loving God whose praises we will sing forever:

> Oh for a thousand tongues to sing
> My great Redeemer's praise,
> The glories of my God and King,
> The triumphs of His grace!
>
> — Charles Wesley

EPILOGUE

During the years I have ministered at the broadcasting network in the Holy Land, my wife, Virginia, and I have traveled to Israel over a hundred times. For me personally, the single most thrilling place on this entire earth isn't even featured in the world's travel brochures. You might be thinking, "Is George's special place Jerusalem, the Sea of Galilee, the Garden Tomb, the Upper Room, or perhaps Mt. Zion?" No, my favorite place is none of those blessed places.

There is a rugged hill between Mt. Carmel and Galilee which overlooks scores of miles of flat fields. It is the location of King Solomon's military stronghold, and it is called *Har' Meggido*, from which the Bible site of Armageddon is named. *Har' Meggido* is where the final and most catastrophic battle of all time will be waged.

The Battle of Armageddon will be Satan's all-out drive to permanently rule this world. Millions will be slain, and then suddenly the great window of heaven will open up in the skies above. Appearing there for all the world to see will be Jesus Christ, sitting on a white horse and leading the armies of heaven. No longer the little baby in the manger, the suffering martyr dying on the cross, or the scarred resurrected Lord, His eyes will be like a flame of fire, His head will carry many crowns, and on His thigh will be written, "King of Kings and Lord of Lords." Our Messiah will return to this earth to stop the war of all wars. (See Revelation 19:11-20:3.)

King Jesus will instantly stop the bloody war and chain Satan and his demons for a thousand years. This will be the dramatic opening of the *Millennium*. Please don't confuse this blessed prophetic event with what the media and some teachers have called "Y2K" or a "new millennium," which began January 1, 2000, and pales by comparison. No, the Millennium I am referring to is the biblical 1,000-year reign of Jesus of Nazareth on the earth.

To inaugurate the book of Revelation's Millennium, our wonderful Lord Jesus will return to earth, descending through the air with His heavenly army and a host of the saints. He will set foot on the same mountain (Mount of Olives) from which He ascended into heaven in A.D. 33, very probably returning to land on the exact same spot. He will then move across the Valley of Kidron, through the now-sealed Golden Gate of Jerusalem, and directly on to Mt. Zion. Then He will sit upon His throne to rule with certain blessed saints like David, the man after God's own heart, for 1,000 years (Jeremiah 30:9, Ezekiel 34:23-24 and Ezekiel 37:24-25.)

EVANGELISM IS STILL KEY

During this paradise-like, 1,000 years of glory, sinlessness, joy, and plenty, will there cease to be a need for evangelism, preaching, and spiritual warnings? No! The Bible says there will be an ongoing need for evangelistic work to be done by believers during Jesus' reign. Why? There will be people on the earth who have yet to decide whether or not to receive Jesus as Lord and Savior.

To understand this more clearly, let's go back to the beginning. God created mankind in the Garden of Eden because He longed for a trustworthy bride. He wanted a free-thinking partner on earth, not some mindless robot. So He bravely gave humans free will in order to develop a bride who would *choose* Him and yearn to do right.

Adam walked with God in the cool of the day in Eden. His special garden had absolutely everything. There was no sin, pain, hunger, or want. But what happened? Satan entered in the form of a serpent and tempted Adam and Eve to violate God's one restriction, saying, "Surely God doesn't mean what He says." But, of course, God always means what He says, and they were driven from paradise by their own sin.

The Lord forgave Adam and Eve and blessed them with sons. But some years later, sin again fostered rebellion. So He brought a great flood on the earth and restarted humanity with the righteous family of Noah. However, it wasn't long before we see God's wrath burst into flames in the sin-crazed people of Sodom. Sadly, He had to wipe out all of the inhabitants except for Lot, his wife, and his two daughters, whom He spared because of Abraham's intercession on their behalf.

Shocking abandonment of Jesus' righteousness on the order of Sodom is occurring now around the earth and will continue to do so until Jesus Christ's return. But it will also occur one more time near the end of the Jesus Millennium. A great rebellion against righteousness will arise from the children of those who survive Armageddon and refuse the gift of salvation in Jesus Christ.

Millions of children who are born during Jesus' reign, while Satan is bound, will need to be evangelized. Many theologians believe that the Millennium will begin with believers only. But believers or not, there will be those who will bear children during this period, and these children must accept Jesus as their Savior. Ultimately, the Bible tells us that many will reject the truth, and they will be deceived by Satan after he is loosed.

Although there will be great security, equality, prosperity, and peace, there will still be those who forsake Jesus and His forgiveness for the rebellion and evil in their hearts. Is that inconceivable? It shouldn't be. Remember that the first rebellion against God started in heaven with Satan and thousands of his followers.

ISRAEL'S DELIVERANCE

Do you remember the 144,000 Jewish "super-evangelists" who will proclaim the Good News during the Tribulation and on into the Millennium years? (See Revelation 14:1-7.) We are already seeing the beginning of a great spiritual transformation in thousands of Jews and have witnessed signs of Israel's spiritual awakening for the past fifty years. It is breathtaking!

For generations hundreds of ancient prophecies about Israel lay fallow and uncertain, like so much dead ink on old, dusty paper. Then earlier in this century, like the ponderous first stage of a rocket launch, the fulfillment of a few of those prophecies began to unfold. Slowly but surely the Hebrew people began coming back to the Holy Land. (See Jeremiah 23:3; Zechariah 8:7-8.) Finally, "stage two" ignited when Israel was restored as a nation. (See Luke 21:29-31.) This monumental biblical occurrence set off an astonishing kaleidoscope of current events, one upon the other! Jesus said, **When these things begin to come to pass, then look up for your redemption draweth nigh** (Luke 21:28).

Most of these prophetic happenings, which are moving off the pages of prophecy right into the pages of contemporary history, are occurring on the Middle East stage. And these events pop with ever increasing frequency as the time for Jesus' return approaches. One of the major prophecies is found in Luke 21:24, where Jesus prophesied that Jerusalem would be trampled by Gentiles until the times of the Gentiles are fulfilled. Those times were fulfilled in 1967 when, on the final day of the Six Day War, the Israeli army fought its way to retake the occupied segment of old Jerusalem and the Temple Mount.

Weeping Jewish soldiers and Rabbis splashed joyful tears against the Wailing Wall, a part of the old temple. Nearly two millennia had ticked off, but suddenly Jerusalem was back under Jewish control. Because of multiple fulfillments of Bible prophecy in modern-day Israel, the eminent historian and philosopher, Dr. Arnold Toynbee, says that mankind now stands at the edge of time.

Just a few months after the Six Day War, I stood one Friday at sundown and watched a "party" the like of which I had never dreamed! Hundreds upon hundreds of Jews came flying through every street, crevice, and alley. They poured jubilantly—yes, explosively—into the hastily built "temple" they had improvised at the Wailing Wall. Why were they so excited? Because their cry through the centuries—"Next year, Jerusalem!"—had finally come to pass. They were experiencing God's promise of old:

> Behold, I will save My people from the land
> of the east and from the land of the west;
> I will bring them back, and they shall dwell in the
> midst of Jerusalem. They shall be My people and I will
> be their God, in truth and righteousness. Zechariah 8:7-8 NKJV

ISRAEL'S TRANSFORMATION

When the Jews began to return to Israel, field irrigation was nearly nonexistent. The land was a scraggly, brown desert wilderness for as far as the eye could see. When you looked at it in those early years, you wondered: *Why would anyone ever want to return to this forlorn, barren place?* But God buried in the deepest atom of every Jew a "little magnet" that compels them toward Israel's ancient soil.

Some twelve years after Israel's modern settlers had been laboring on the land, I flew to the Holy Land. By then, 300 million little trees had been planted throughout the country. The Jews have a national "thing" about this. They plant a tree for you if it's your birthday, your anniversary, your graduation day, your wedding, or in remembrance of a loved one. As we drove through a countryside where irrigation systems had been installed, I looked out of the car window and could hardly believe my eyes! I marveled at the sight of lush groves of banana trees, citrus, cotton, grain, and vegetables. The newly wooded hills had turned green and flowers bloomed again.

Israel's incredible physical transformation in such a few years shook me up. It was like resurrection! It was a direct fulfillment of Isaiah's prophecy:

> *I will plant in the wilderness the cedar and the acacia tree,*
> *the myrtle and the oil tree; I will set in the desert the*
> *cypress tree and the pine and the box tree together,*
>
> *That they may see and know, and consider and understand*
> *together, that the hand of the Lord has done this, and the*
> *Holy One of Israel has created it. Isaiah 41:19-20 NKJV*

I shouted to my driver, "What a change! It's beginning to look like the Garden of Eden!" Little did I know as I spoke it, my words were fulfilling an ancient scripture.

> *For the Lord will comfort Zion, He will comfort all her waste*
> *places; He will make her wilderness like Eden, and her desert*
> *like the garden of the Lord; joy and gladness will be found in it,*
> *thanksgiving and the voice of melody. Isaiah 51:3 NKJV*

The prophet Ezekiel was given a vision of the Jews scattered throughout the world as a vast field of dry bones. When he prophesied to them as the Lord had commanded him, he saw them supernaturally come together as a skeleton and then living, vibrant flesh appeared (Ezekiel 37). Today, God has not only connected the dry bones and laid on new flesh of Israel, but He has obviously begun to breathe His breath into her nostrils. For there she sits today, not only alive and lovely, but spiritually awakening.

After their rejection of the Messiah, the Bible repeatedly speaks of a season in which God's beloved Jews will be spiritually blind. Why? Paul tells us in Romans 9:31-32 NKJV:

> *Israel, pursuing the law of righteousness,*
> *has not attained to the law of righteousness.*
> *Why? Because they did not seek it by faith, but as it were, by*
> *the works of the law. For they stumbled at that stumbling stone.*

The stumbling stone, of course, is Jesus of Nazareth. Paul then goes on to remind us that because of the nation's rejection of Messiah-Jesus, we Gentiles were blessed in our New Testament faith. He writes:

> *I say then, have they* [the Jews] *stumbled that they should fall?*
> *Certainly not! But through their fall, to provoke*
> *them to jealousy, salvation has come to the Gentiles.*
> *Now if their fall is riches for the world, and*
> *their failure riches for the Gentiles, how much*
> *more their fullness!* Romans 11:11-12 NKJV

How perfect are the ways of our heavenly Father!

NEW EYES TO SEE

Since their forefathers rejected Jesus as Messiah, the Jews have experienced a horrible darkness in spiritual matters, and they have suffered terribly. Their persecution over the centuries has been devastating. Many of these dear Jews understand their persecution only in terms of racism. They do not see that they are God's chosen people who brought forth the Messiah Jesus, and they are like the unbelieving Gentiles who have vacuous holes in the center of their being only God can fill. Every human being has a built-in sense of life after death down in that secret place. Yet so many struggle to fog over this innate sense of eternity, trying in a thousand ways to kill that ticking clock inside. But each of us will soon "awaken from death" to face a real and a living God!

There is a delusion that Satan and his demons propagate in the minds of mankind that makes some act as though they'll never die, trying to convince themselves that the little motor in their chest will never stop. But the greatest shock will come in that moment when they "wake up dead" to discover eternal existence is a reality.

Yes, everyone is going to have eternal existence whether they like it or not. But the quality of that infinite existence is set by each person's decision during this present finite lifetime concerning Jesus Christ. God prepared a 66-book "Road Map to Heaven" so every human being could know how to find success in life, both for now and in eternity. It won't help the foolish to say, "I didn't know!" after it's one heartbeat too late and they stand without excuse before God. Each human will either spend eternity in the very presence of God or separated from Him in eternal darkness and torment, unable even to die. We choose our eternal destiny when we reject or accept Jesus Christ.

Though it is hard to fathom, there will be multitudes who will not accept Jesus' salvation during the Millennium. So our King has ordained one final confrontation to guarantee spiritual integrity. He will conduct one last spiritual and moral test before He carries His bride into the New Jerusalem. How will He do this?

At the end of the 1,000-year reign of Jesus, God will loose Satan from his millennial chains, and the devil will go straight to war against Jesus and His people again. Most of the unsaved, rebellious people will follow him. But God will destroy them with fire from heaven and condemn Satan and his followers to their final destiny: the lake of fire. Once the devil and his demons are gone forever, the New Jerusalem will come down out of heaven, and the faithful in Christ will dwell with Him forever.

Now I saw a new heaven and a new earth,
for the first heaven and the first earth had
passed away. Also there was no more sea.
Then I, John, saw the holy city, New Jerusalem,
coming down out of heaven from God,
prepared as a bride adorned for her husband.

And I heard a loud voice from heaven saying,
Behold, the tabernacle of God is with men, and He
will dwell with them, and they shall be His people.
God Himself will be with them and be
their God.   Revelation 21:1-3 NKJV

Before this fantastic event, however, we will see that evangelism, preaching, and discipleship will continue right up until
Satan's final defeat! (See Revelation 21:24.) Also, remember
God's neverending love for the Jews? He will deal with His chosen
people just a little bit differently than the Gentiles during the
Millennium. They are forever His chosen people, and the Bible
tells us that when Jesus returns, the Jews will see Him, mourn
over their rejection of Him, and receive His Holy Spirit.

And I will pour on the house of David and on the inhabitants
of Jerusalem the Spirit of grace and supplication; then
they will look on Me whom they pierced. Yes, they will
mourn for Him as one mourns for his only son, and grieve
for Him as one grieves for a firstborn.   Zechariah 12:10 NKJV

These Jews will be powerful witnesses and evangelists throughout the Millennium, and all of their land will be restored. The
Lord will also assign many other believers to evangelize and
teach those unsaved throughout the earth. We will say, "It is
the time to take the kingdom; rise up, you strong. **The
kingdoms of this world have become the kingdoms of our
Lord and of His Christ, and He shall reign forever and**

ever (Revelation 11:15.) We have a great mission to reach the lost right now—and in the Millennium!

In the meantime, we must look up, for our Lord and Savior will soon split the sky and come once again to dwell with us. Hallelujah!

> My brother, wait! From Zion's hill,
> Or soon, or late—arrive He will!
> Enrobed in light, He'll blow His horn,
> Drive the night, and light the morn;
> Unchain the earth, renew its youth,
> And give rebirth to life and truth.
> Look up the hill, dream on thy dream;
> For come He will.

> Philip M. Raskin, from *The Sentinel,* a widely circulated Jewish weekly, 1953

About the Author

George Otis Sr., the founder of High Adventure Ministries, pursued a career in the secular business world which eventually led to his appointment as a chief executive for LearJet and Dr. Bill Lear. Years later, following a powerful conversion to Christ, George recounted his testimony in a book, where he describes the experience of walking with Jesus as "High Adventure." He then founded a publishing business, Bible Voice, Inc., which produced the entire Bible on tapes and records for the first time. He is the author of twelve books.

High Adventure Ministries was birthed in 1973 as an outreach to bless George's beloved Israel by bringing thousands of pilgrims to the Holy Land. During one such tour, the opportunity to touch Israel and the entire Middle East through radio and television was presented. Thus, the Voice of Hope World Network was born on September 9, 1979. The television station was later gifted to Pat Robertson and CBN.

"As I ponder the future of High Adventure," George says, "I don't think of transmitters, studios, or eloquent sermons, but millions of lives being touched through the Voice of Hope World Network."

High Adventure Ministries consists of sixteen very large world band, AM and FM radio stations, which are heard on every continent, reach over 250 nations, and are presented in seventeen languages. High Adventure is also actively using satellite and the Internet to further the Gospel. This broadcast outreach is now heading into its twentieth year of bringing in the final harvest and preparing the way for the Lord's return.

To contact George Otis Sr., you may
write him at the following address:

High Adventure Ministries
696 Verdemont Circle
Simi Valley, CA 93065

Additional copies of this book and other book titles
from ALBURY PUBLISHING are
available at your local bookstore.

ALBURY PUBLISHING
P. O. Box 470406
Tulsa, Oklahoma 74147-0406

For a complete list of our titles,
visit us at our website:
www.alburypublishing.com

For international and Canadian orders,
please contact:

Access Sales International
2448 East 81st Street
Suite 4900
Tulsa, Oklahoma 74137
Phone 918-523-5590   Fax 918-496-2822